# WHO BROKE THE GIRL?

CRISTINA COSTANTINO

Copyright © 2015 Waking Works Press

All rights reserved.

ISBN: 978-0-692-48163-9

☆
## DEDICATION

For every little girl or boy who has ever felt fear.

☆
## CONTENTS

Introduction: A FIRST START            1

WHAT HAPPENED TO THE GIRL             3

WHERE THE GIRL RAN TO SEE            83

WHEN THE GIRL RAN STILL             165

Conclusion: AN END TO HER START     237

☆
## ACKNOWLEDGMENTS

Thank you to everyone who has helped me
create this life and these words.

☆
## INTRODUCTION: A FIRST START

This girl, when she was a 12-year-old girl, sat herself down in her hard seat, at her wooden desk, in her house that couldn't keep the cold out. She pressed the sharp tip of her pencil to the first straight line of her blank paper, and waited for her words to come. The pencil knew the story the words would tell. There was a girl. A strong girl who went out to travel a hard road by herself. A strong girl, on a hard road, who faced cold fear by herself. Who took care of herself. Who found courage for herself.

The tip of this girl's pencil stayed sharp, and her paper stayed blank. She was blank. She was 12. She hadn't gone any farther, down her own road, than the road that circled the small block that her cold house was on. She hadn't gone any further, down her own road, then to face down the fears of the family she lived with in that cold house. The family that was too afraid to let this girl off that block. She put her pencil down, and forgot the girl on the road, without ever realizing she was that girl. A girl who would have to wait for her words until her road got longer.

Over the next 25 years, while this girl forgot about the strong girl on a road, her steps took her far. Driving this girl in one direction, before she pushed it in different directions. Running her straight into her fears, before turning, and breaking her on her happiest dreams. A road that dropped low, low enough to force this girl to wake up, before she dropped too low to get back up. A road that lifted this girl up higher, high enough so she could lift herself up higher, to reach her highest self. After 25 years, once she ran her road down, the words about a strong girl on a road came to this girl.

WHO BROKE THE GIRL?

☆

PART ONE
# WHAT HAPPENED TO THE GIRL
(YEARS: 0 - 26)

WHO BROKE THE GIRL?

☆
## THE GIRL

Before words explain how the girl kept breaking down, while on her road, words will explain the girl, back when she was a little girl. When she first learned how to feel broken. Back before all that came changed her into someone she didn't know, and before she could see clearly enough to become the girl who was always inside of her. Before all of that, the girl saw everything through a rosy tint, even though she had to see herself through so much that wasn't so good. Through all of it she still believed everything she dreamed up could be hers one day. Only later, after enough dreams broke apart on her, would she lose that lens and start to lose herself. Forcing her to look at everything that wasn't so good, so she could clear it out and see her dreams again.

The girl saw too much through big, rounded eyes that looked too serious too much of the time. She was pretty, except when she didn't feel pretty enough. She didn't take up a lot of space, but she always wanted to take up less space. The girl wasn't a tall girl, but she always felt too tall next to someone who wasn't as tall. She wasn't a short girl, but she always felt too short next to someone who wasn't as short. Her dark hair was too curly to be straight, so they made it curlier, when she really just wanted it to be straighter. Her heart-shaped lips had a natural pout to them, and they never could fake a smile right.

    She was from here because she was born here, but she always felt like she was from back there, where the ones who had her had been before they came over. Everything back there was different from everything over here. Back where everything was older and smaller, everyone made everything out of nothing, and stood by what they thought was right, even when it was wrong. Everything that was different, from back there, came over here with them, and all the families that were like them, the ones that were always with them. The girl lived here now, but she lived every day as if she was living back there then. So she never did feel like she belonged here, even though she never did belong back there.

    Since they weren't from here, everyone over here thought they could never understand what was being told to them. The girl saw everyone look down at them, and then over towards her to tell her, so she could tell them. She always told everyone – "They can understand you." But back before they learned to understand, back before she was born here, they didn't understand when to expect her. So when the girl came they couldn't get past the fear that she brought them. Fear because she came too early, for them, even though she came right when she was supposed to be there. Fear that something with her was wrong, even though everything about her was right. Later, farther down her road, the girl would come too early two more times. Bringing fear with her, even though when she would come would be right when someone needed her.

When the girl came, that first time, they named her. A hard name that wasn't heard right. Written down with more than it was meant to have, loading her down with more than she needed, when she already had more than most. Her name, when it had to be written, was always going to be a hard one to get right. She would work hard her whole life to lose the extra load she was given to carry. Never giving up, not even when something was hard enough to give up on. Sticking with what she believed in, no matter how hard it was to stick with.

The girl, who stood by her beliefs, wasn't stuck on the first name that called her out from them. It was too long, and had too many breaks, making it too hard to say. She could hear how it didn't flow easily, and see how everyone tripped over its hard edges. She knew, without anyone saying, that no one wanted to say her whole name. So she made it shorter, in a way that flowed the way she wanted to back then. It would stay that way for a while, before changing with her when she changed. The changing faces that came into her life, which she would change with, would keep changing it on her. She always flowed with them and those names, until neither fit her any longer.

The girl with so many names won't have one here. To know them won't help know her. The only way to know the girl is to hear how she started out, whom she knew, and who she was along the way. The only way to understand the girl is to see what's inside of her, the same things inside of everyone she brought into her life. The only way to care for the girl is to feel what was done to her, everything she did to herself.

WHO BROKE THE GIRL?

☆
## THE GIRL'S LESSONS FOR LIFE

When the girl was a little girl she learned fear. Fear filled her when their anger tensed in the air, in the days before their yells filled the cold house. She knew tension would fill the silence, until the silence couldn't hold back the anger. Fear filled her when she lay in bed upstairs and heard their yells being thrown around downstairs. She knew they couldn't hear what was behind the yells they were throwing. Fear filled her when she was sat downstairs with her sister who was bigger and her brother who was smaller, to watch their faces twist out their yells through the darkest part of their night. She knew the only thing a yell changed was the person yelling.

Fear filled her when the men, who looked official, came on the nights the yells came out the loudest; telling them they had to stop yelling because the small block didn't want to hear them. She knew they didn't know how to stop the yells that came from too many fears, across too many years. Fear filled her when the one official, looking over sadly, said they had to stop yelling because small ears shouldn't have to hear them. She knew they couldn't stop, too afraid of what could happen if they weren't there to hear them. Fear filled her when their yells left tension in the air, in the days after a round of anger stopped yelling. She knew the yells that had been released hadn't released any of the fear behind them. Fear filled her in the days after the tension lifted. She knew to fear the next round that would start the week after next.

Her lessons were learned. The little girl who was full of love learned to love full of fear; accepting the fear so she wouldn't have to give up the love. The little girl who was wise enough to know a yell was never heard, never learned to speak out; worried anything spoken too loud would return a yell. The little girl who wanted to live in peace learned what she needed didn't matter, even to the ones it was supposed to matter to; seeing that everyone else mattered more, she came to believe she mattered less.

When the little girl became a little older, the rounds she had grown to fear grew further apart. Their yells weren't thrown at each other as much now. They joined together to be thrown at them. Yells hit the girl when she whispered her sadness. The sadness that made them afraid they weren't a happy family. Her sadness, they yelled, hurt their happy times, so they needed her to be happy. The girl heard she had been made to bring them their good times, so she made herself the good one. Her sister, who was becoming too big for their house, was as good as she could be, which was never good enough. Their yells threw most of their fears at her.

Once the girl wasn't as little, even though she still wasn't big, she was forced into those yells. She had to help her sister. She used her small strength to pull her stronger father off her bigger sister, that one time the two sisters crashed his car down a wet road. His fear made him so afraid that he knocked her sister down to the ground, and then stood over her to slap all of his fear out on her. She had to help her mother. She used her small frame to pull her mother's weakened frame up those times her bigger sister ran from the yells knocking her down in their house to the support holding her up in her friend's house. Leaving the girl behind to feel their grasps of pain and be hit with their cries to bring her bigger sister back to them.

Her lessons were learned. The girl who could feel what everyone was feeling learned that no one could feel for her, so she hid her sadness and tried to give everyone the happiness they wanted. The girl who was always good learned to feel guilty for not being good enough; so she made herself too good for her own good. The girl who used all of her strength to hold up anyone she loved who needed holding never learned to hold back enough strength for herself; so she would always fall when someone she was holding up dropped her.

Her sister left their house when she was big enough, but the girl had already left her behind. She'd had enough of being left behind by her. She was getting big enough to make her own push to leave everything in this life behind, but she still wasn't strong enough to do it. When they drove her anywhere her heart would always push her to open the door and jump out onto the road. The push was strong, but her fear of what was out there that might hit her was stronger. So fear beat her heart, and she stopped its push.

By then she had her own friend's house to run to, but the girl always asked to run before she ran anywhere. Her ask was sometimes given a simple yes, but most of the time she was given her smaller brother to carry there with her. Once, she was given no words, just a strong push backwards. Followed by a hard slap right, then left, right, left, right, left. She never knew where those slaps came from. She always knew what the fear was behind the others.

There was the hard slap of fear that hit her when he thought she was lost, that time she left the small block to play one block over. Then the hard slap of fear that hit her when he didn't think she was telling the truth, the time she didn't know her card would report her success wasn't as good as the time before. And the last time the hard right, left, right, left swing of slaps came back. When the girl didn't come back on time, the night she was let out to have a fun time. She wasn't back because she hadn't spoken up in time, too afraid to stop everyone else's fun and ask to be taken back. She only lost the fear of using her voice later that night. Only, she didn't try to stop anyone then either. With every slap given, she yelled – "Go ahead. Give me more." The girl felt every slap she got, and she felt her power.

Her lessons were learned. The girl who wanted to lighten up like everyone else learned to have fun while carrying the heavy weight pulling her down. The girl who always told the truth learned her truth didn't stand a chance next to someone else's truth about her. The girl who always wanted to do what was right learned to punish herself more than she was being punished, when something was done that wasn't right by someone else.

They never meant for the girl to learn those lessons. They'd never learned the lessons you're meant to teach. The girl never met the older ones who'd raised them without teaching them those lessons. Those older ones had stayed back there, back where they'd come from. There was only the one time that the girl saw one of them. She saw the one who'd mothered her mother in the middle of the night, after she left the place she'd lived her entire life and before she'd gone into the light. She sat there watching over her, and the girl woke to see her. She looked like she wanted to help, but the girl didn't know how to handle this kind of help.

## CRISTINA COSTANTINO

Seeing her made the girl feel what she had already learned to feel too well, and her fear overwhelmed her.

WHO BROKE THE GIRL?

☆
## HOW THE GIRL ESCAPED

The girl didn't know how to be helped, but that didn't stop her from crying out for help. She never cried out loud to anyone who could hear those cries. She always cried out silently, to anyone in the universe who could hear that. When help came, from wherever it was coming from, she could never see its helping hand, and it always took something from her. Getting help brought up guilt, and the more she got the more of that she felt.

Her own body tried its best to help her. Her ears, the ones forced to hear the hard words being yelled, tried to make everyone see the pain she was full of. Time and again, her ears poured out the sickness that was stuck inside of her. Time and again, they cleaned up what was coming out, but never stopped putting in what was causing it. Then a time came when the girl's ears tried harder to silence everyone around her. The father who didn't know how to stop putting his fear in her, felt fear for her, and he knew to rush her to someone for help. Just in time to stop her ears from deafening the world around her. That type of peace wasn't meant for her.

The girl used her eyes to escape. They read about the worlds she found in other people's words. She read many words that told her many stories about many other girls. These stories told her about happy girls, strong girls, funny girls, pretty girls, and smart girls. These stories told her about happy families, big families, old families, young families, and strong families. She read their stories in every room of her house, through every hour of this life. The girl escaped into those stories, and she escaped to the building that housed all types of stories. Happy walking through its rows, she was happiest when checking out a fresh pile of its stories. There were plenty of them to help her escape plenty of hours.

When a story didn't give her the escape she had in mind, she would escape into her mind to change the story. She could always dream up new sections to replace the ones she didn't like, but never could imagine a happier ending. Not to any one of all those stories. The girl's mind replayed these stories while her eyes were open to the light.

## WHO BROKE THE GIRL?

But when her eyes closed in the dark her fears took her over. They took her to places where no girl should go, and where no girl wanted to get stuck. So she always came back, even though she felt stuck in this life.

When the weight holding her down got too heavy the girl's mind would get light. It pushed out and up, bringing her high above everything weighing her down, and she would look down to observe herself in this life. Her mind could escape the heaviness for a moment, the heaviness that the girl still couldn't escape any other way.

She saw what she thought was an escape, but it was one that wasn't hers to have. The girl saw how easy it was being a boy in this family, which seemed so much easier than being a girl. Making the boy happy seemed to matter, and when the boy shouted it was all that mattered. The boy didn't have to work hard for what he wanted, being a boy just worked. The girl did her work and his, but started doing it with a shorter name. Everyone started calling her by half her name, the half that sounded like a boy that mattered.

The girl who didn't know she mattered started to run to a new friend that mattered to her. She wanted this friend to be her first friend, one that was as close as a sister. The friend already had two sisters that she didn't have to leave behind, so she didn't have space for another one. She had space for a friend, so she made the girl her first friend, right after her sisters. She still became the girl's first friend before anyone.

The first friend's family had come from back there, where the girl's family had come from, but they were the big, happy family the girl wanted to be from. The first friend was just like the girl wanted to be, the part of her that she didn't know how to be, except when she was with her. The girl found a good escape with her first friend. With her she could push her sadness aside, put her weight down, and be lifted up by laughter. With her first friend the girl could be herself, only with her though, never by herself.

The girl felt safe with her, a safety that came from being one of two. She liked how she looked with the first friend who always saw her. Even though no one else could see her when she was with her. She hid next to the first friend who always walked next to her. She hid behind the first friend who she always put first. The girl hid herself where it felt safe, for the six years they stayed first friends. For all those years they walked next to each other every hour, every day. They talked to each other every hour, every night. They went with each other to everything, every time.

There was only one day that the girl's first friend wasn't there to walk next to her, and she couldn't escape the fear that came with being on her own. Walking by herself, hugging a wall to her right, she couldn't see the threat coming her way. She turned a corner. The girl was walked into, and the girl didn't walk away. She felt fear, but she refused to lose face, so she stood her ground. A yell was thrown straight at her. The girl didn't throw any back, but she didn't whisper herself back down. Her words, spoken loudly, drove a closed fist to be thrown straight into her face.

She would have thrown herself, but she couldn't go that far down this path. One of the older ones that was there to guide them, jumped up to help her. The girl didn't feel that help, all she felt was a weight holding her back. The girl used all of her strength to push forward, and her eyes threw her power into the face of what she feared. Protected by no one, the large girl that had hit her pressed back, afraid of the force she saw inside the girl. The girl won that day, and she started to feel her power.

After she took her hit from fear, the girl took her punishment without any fear. She waited for it knowing she deserved it for doing something that wasn't right. She didn't expect her punishment to come with praise. Praise came from all of the other young ones who had been walked into, and from all of the older ones who were tired of watching it. Taking this praise felt strange for the girl who didn't know how to take anything that was good for her.

The girl, who didn't know how to take what was good when it was given, was good at giving, and everything she gave was good. She always gave her first friend everything she had to give. Her first friend always took everything she gave her. To celebrate her, on her birthday one year, the girl gave her a sign of their faith that she could wear. The girl loved giving this to her, and her first friend loved the look of what she gave her. So she got two of the same sign and gave her faith to her sisters, so all three could wear them together.

The girl wouldn't let herself feel how this felt, and she couldn't tell her first friend how this felt. Feeling like she didn't matter, she made herself understand. She needed her first friend to be like a sister, but her first friend didn't need her, not as much as her sisters. The girl wasn't one of the two, so she had to come in second to the two. This time, like every time, her first friend did what she felt like doing, the girl felt what they both felt, and the first friend bother with her feelings.

WHO BROKE THE GIRL?

☆
## **LIVING INSIDE THE GIRL**

The girl felt shame. She had shame over having a family that was different from other families. She had shame from a block that heard when they weren't a happy family. She had her father's shame when she picked him up from the officials after they took him away for one night. Her shame lived inside of her along with fear and guilt. No one could feel what she felt, and no one asked the girl how she felt. She could never tell anyone any of it, so she put the sharp tip of her pencil to the first straight line of her blank paper, once again. This time hard words came. From left to right, one

line to the next, one page to the last filled with the words she was filled with – "I wish I was dead."
She knew this wish, worded again and again, was only words. She always knew, but she knew for sure the time fear threw its power behind those words. That time the girl, who always did what she was told, was found out for doing something other than what she had told them. Done so she could have fun with everyone. The high of her freedom dropped, and trapped her in her guilt. Fear saw this was its time to turn her wish into more than just words, and her guilt wanted to let fear win.

It hit her hard, but the girl's strength hit back harder. They found her then, and saw the blade in her hand, but they knew what she knew. She was stronger. This wouldn't be the only time fear came on this strong to use that wish against her. One more time later in time, then one more time soon after that, but then never again. After that, this death wish died, but that wouldn't stop the girl from trying to kill off her life with the way she lived it.

The girl had a second wish, a different one that she stopped wishing for almost as soon as she started. She wished that when she was no longer a girl, she would have two girls and three boys of her own. She wished to make her own big, happy family. For a time, this wish made her thoughts happy. She held on to it until the day she had a new thought, one that came from no other thoughts she was having. One that came with a feeling, from deep inside, that told her it was more than just a passing thought. She was struck with the knowledge that this wish wasn't hers to have. The road that other girls took, to get to their happy families, wasn't going to be the same for her. That thought never left her, but the wish did.

The girl had a third wish that she'd wished for from the beginning, and that she'd make come true by the end. But not until later then she'd hoped, and only to end sooner then she'd planned. She wished they would take her back down the road they'd taken, and bring her back to live where they were from. Back where their family had more family, and everyone understood them. Back there she imagined they would be happy, and she could be happy. But back when she could only dream up parts of someone else's story, wishing for this didn't change anything. One day, after she stopped wishing for it, this wish would come back to her, and she would do everything to get herself back there.

The girl would have to wait for that day. These days she felt happiest with her first friend. Inside and out the girl cared about her first friend more than others, so she took more care with her, more than she took with others. Other than her sisters, she knew her first friend cared about her the most, but she still took more care with others. The wise girl understood why things were this way. Showing someone how much you cared made that one feel they could show you less, safe that they would still have all of yours. Knowing this didn't stop the girl. She understood, and she didn't care, she wanted to keep caring. Not for everyone. She never cared for everyone she came across in life, but she would always take a lot of care with anyone she cared for, and she would always care if they didn't care about her.

It may not seem like the girl stood as tall as everyone around her, but the girl could stand taller. She first showed how strong she was when she was at the school that was in the middle. Back before she stood her ground against the fear that struck her, she'd shown everyone a glimpse of what she stood for. Back when everyone she called a friend had followed each other away from one of the ones they had all once stood with. At first she followed along too, agreeing with the sentiment. Then the day came when everyone turned around and followed each other back to that friend. The girl didn't stand for what everyone stood for, so she stopped following. She chose to stand tall without anyone, and pushed her way straight through the crowd that shared one mentality.

The girl didn't care what everyone stood for. She cared about what she stood for on the inside, what she knew was good. The girl didn't know how what she had inside of her stayed standing, with everything that kept falling on her, but she knew it wouldn't run out on her. This hard time would run out for her. She knew that time would change everything, if she could hold on long enough. So she waited through this time, and looked forward to the next. To when she could leave all of these hard times behind, to reach her time, when happiness would shine.

☆
## THE GOOD THROUGH THE BAD

Before words tell what happened to the girl after she left this life, there are words for the other parts of this life. There were good times, which is what made the hard times even harder. Her family, the one that made her feel sad, wasn't a bad family. They ate family dinners together, smiled together, swam together, wrestled together, and watched movies together. The family that had come from back there always gathered with all the other families from back there. To picnic together, cook together, go to the beach together, play together, and laugh together. The whole time she lived that life they lived part of it as a happy family.

Her father, who was scary when he was angry, wasn't mean. The bad things that had happened to him when he was little, that he hadn't let go of when he'd gotten bigger, were still hurting him. The fear from what he'd lived through made him too afraid to let them live, out of a fear that he would lose them. His breaks from the jumps he'd had to make too young, made him afraid to let them jump, out of a fear of them falling. That fear drove the anger the girl hated in her father, and it drove her fear of him. But this fear was no match for the love she felt from him, which was the same as the love she felt for her.

Her mother, who couldn't protect them from fear, wasn't weak. She had left behind everything in her life back there, where she had learned to work hard and have faith, for the promise of a better life over here. She worked hard to try to make this life look better than what she'd left behind. She followed close behind them, every minute of every day, and worked hard to clean every surface, so no one would see the mess their family made. Her fear of his anger, even when there was no anger to fear, made her jump on them too quick, whenever they made any little jump. The fear the girl hated in her mother drove the anger she felt for her. But this fear was no match for the love she felt from her, which was the same as the love she felt for her.

Her sister, who was bigger, always jumped. Not far, but far enough to scare the girl. Before she left them to start her

## WHO BROKE THE GIRL?

life, the girl saw every jump and tried to stop her before they saw them. They tried to control her, but she always broke away, however she could. After she left she came back for all of her school breaks, and the girl always feared everything that would break while she was back with them. The girl knew she could be good enough to lighten the anger in the house when her sister was gone, but she couldn't stop her sister, so she couldn't stop the anger that came up when she was back with them. The girl's anger at her pushed down her love for her, and kept her from treating her like a sister. It would be decades before the support she got from her showed the girl what she'd been missing, and the love that had always been between them turned them back into sisters again.

Her brother, who was smaller and never made to work hard for what he wanted, made the girl feel the weight of responsibility. She had to take care of him since it mattered that he was smaller, but because he was a boy it would have mattered even if he were bigger. She was meant to carry him wherever she went. He was sweet when he was small, but she could see, even then, how they were spoiling him. Their fear of his cries, when he didn't get what he wanted, made them jump to give him everything before he even cried out. She knew she had to take him with her everywhere, but she stopped carrying him anywhere after she left. But the responsibility she carried for him made her feel the guilt of letting him get spoiled. Only much later, after this story ends, once she went back and helped him could she let go of her guilt and understand that his lessons were his to learn, not hers to take on.

All the wrong lessons, given by the ones who loved her, weren't the only ones the girl learned. She learned how to be good, and would always value what was good, even though she never learned that she deserved someone to be good to her. She learned how to take care of others, and would always care if someone needed her care, even though she never learned how to care for herself. She learned to never speak badly of others, and would always think before speaking, even though she never learned how to speak for herself. She learned that how much work you do matters, and always wanted to do good work that mattered, even though she never learned that she mattered more than the work.

When the girl was little she saw how much her father made his work matter. Working hard every hour of every day, like he had since he was too young to work, while fixing everyone's cars for them. She didn't know this father then, since she didn't ever see this father then. She only heard him, and the sound of his anger at the day, during the night. That was all she knew of him. Then the day came when that work stopped.

Instead of doing what he should on that day, he was doing what he could to help. Cleaning out everything that had to be moved out from up high made him fall hard. That day everything broke for him when his back, the one he used to carry all of them, broke on him, forcing him to lie down. After that day he was told he had to stay home with them every day and couldn't fix anything any longer. In the days after it happened she wondered out loud about it. She told everyone that it had happened because she wasn't being good enough. They all smiled, but no one saw that after that day her back took on his pain. It began to split in its own pain every time she had to stand too straight for too long.

After that day her mother had to become stronger. Instead of being a mother who only cleaned inside their house for them, she began to clean outside for others. That didn't stop her mother from cleaning for them, and it didn't make her mother them any less. She cleaned inside during the day, then outside at night. She cooked for them before she left to clean up after everyone else. She came back to them hours after they'd eaten their family dinner, the one she no longer ate with them. From early in the morning until late at night, her mother kept herself moving, working herself to death for them.

This became their way of life. A life that made them worry, and that made the girl feel the added weight of their worries. She worried for her father, who worried because he couldn't carry his family as far as he wanted to on his broken back. She worried for her mother, who had to carry so much on her back that was starting to break under so much weight. She worried for them when they worried about how much it would take to carry their family month-to-month.

She worried about their life, but she didn't see anything wrong with the split in this life, not until she was told that she should. Her pride was split in half when someone else's mother, who didn't know their truth, said the girl had a mother who couldn't clean up after her because she had to clean for others. She didn't say more, but the girl heard how much more she was saying. The girl heard exactly what the other mother wanted her to hear, and she felt exactly what she was meant to feel. She felt split between pride and shame for her mother.

The girl's father worried more than anyone, and his pride wouldn't let him live this kind of life. They'd told him his back wouldn't be strong enough for him to work for the rest of his life. He listened to them for as long as he could, but then his pride, which had been split in half, took over. He found strength inside of him and went out to find work again. He worked for them, and so he could live with his pride.

The girl might have found some balance if there hadn't been so much good mixed in with so much that was so hard on her. Trying to balance between the two, in this one life, kept throwing her off balance. Learning how to balance was the lesson she wouldn't learn early enough. She would keep losing hers in the extremes her life would swing between. Never understanding throughout the years why she couldn't hold on to happiness whenever she found it. After leaving this life behind, she turned away from everything that was weighing her down, without learning how to lift herself up

## WHO BROKE THE GIRL?

the right way, so she would keep carrying the weight of it with her everywhere. Thinking she had left everything hard behind when she left the house on that small block, she would let those hard lessons keep guiding her life.

CRISTINA COSTANTINO

WHO BROKE THE GIRL?

☆
## FIRST PASS AT A NEW LIFE

When it came time for the girl to make a push on her own, she could have gone further, but she wasn't ready to push out that far just yet. Her move may have only moved her to the other side of her same town, but it was a universe she had never known before. That first day, they took her off the road she had been stuck on and left her on a new road, to start her new life. She'd only go back to live with them in short bursts now, when everyone at this university took a break from this life. Those times back were short enough that this new life became her whole life. But while she was in it she didn't break off from them as much as she could have.

## CRISTINA COSTANTINO

They kept coming back for her, to do what she still needed done for her. Twice a week, every week, every year of the four she lived there. The girl had to work, and she had to go back down the road she'd come up to go do that work. She could have worked closer, but she needed more support than anything closer could give. She could have found another way to get there, but she wasn't ready to get there on her own just yet. After the hard hours of work, the girl would jump back into her new life while slamming their door behind her. Every time she needed them they came back for her, and she opened their door back up, not ready to keep it shut behind her.

In-between doors the girl found a good life that she loved living. She loved the freedom she had, in this life, to live it her way. She loved the friends she made, in this life, who all seemed so different from her. She loved her first boy, in this life, and he was good. It was the life she had always wanted. Her first friend, from her first life, never came to see her in this one. She didn't live far away, but they stayed far apart. They'd lived one life stuck side-by-side, and now both needed to live their own lives.

Everything in her life had changed, and the girl lightened up with the change, but she still hadn't change enough. She still called herself half of who she was, the half that sounded like a boy who mattered, and still didn't know she had to make herself matter. Instead, the boy she loved first mattered first to her. She mattered to him, but she knew she would only ever come in second for him. His boys, those on his team with him, would always come first. The girl never let that matter to her. She knew how to be second in one of two. That's where she was safest. What she didn't know was how to be first, that spot scared her.

The boy might not have made the girl matter first to him, but he was still good to her. His love was good for her, and they were good to each other. They always spoke good words and had good fun. The boy's close friends were good guys, and the girl became close friends with their girls, who were all good. They all had plenty of good times together. This was the time she had lived for, when she was living through her hard times.

Despite all that was good in this life, it still held hard times for her. The hard pieces from her past were still living inside of her. In the girl's new life she felt more happiness more of the time, but she couldn't always push back the sadness. It came back to surprise her. It came back to attack her. It came back to remind her. Sadness wouldn't just let itself be forgotten. So the girl lived a happy life, but only during some of this life. The other life, the sad one she still had to go back to, the sad one that still came back to her, was always inside of her.

The boy who was good had lived too good a life to understand her, but he never left her for her sadness. The boy tried to stop her sadness. He told the girl she wasn't just pretty enough for everyone, she was as pretty as everyone. When one of his boys said her hair would look good straight, the boy said he liked the way her curls looked better. The two stayed close, laughing when they were with their friends, and laughing together when it was just the two of them. The boy would hold the girl close, hugging her tight with all of his strength, and he never used any of that strength to hurt her.

When the sadness came on too strong the girl would hide in a corner and curl up tight into herself. She would cry the sadness she didn't want to see any longer out of her, begging to go back to being her happier self. One of these times the wish to stop this life came creeping back, and the girl who couldn't see it tried to sleep away the sadness. What she took wouldn't have done more than knock her out for the night, but the boy came before that happened, and he saw what the girl hadn't. The boy who was good hugged her close, and he used his goodness to stop the wish that wasn't good for her.

This boy always brought the girl out of her sadness and into his good life, even when she had to go back to her other life. When they broke apart for their first few months of sad separation, he made her a tape mixed with music to remind her of their happiness. The girl would listen to his mix of happiness and feel his goodness close to her. During that break she went for a weekend to see him in his good life, and she felt happiness there with him, but could also feel how she didn't belong there. She wouldn't belong anywhere that happy until she could push all the sadness out of her. That didn't stop the girl from believing for the

## WHO BROKE THE GIRL?

first half of this new life, that they would live one happy life together, for all of this life.

This good boy wasn't the only boy who was good to her. There was one who was from her first life. They had been friends back then, but they hadn't been good friends yet. The girl had wanted to be more than friends back then. He hadn't wanted her then, but now that she only wanted him to be a good friend he wanted her to be more. She told him all about her good boy though, so he pushed down his feelings and chose to be her good guy friend. He listened to all of her talk about the boy whose love she wanted, even though he wanted his love to be hers.

He was the good guy friend that came the last time her sadness came back too strong. The time curling up with it wasn't enough for her sadness. He came the last time the wish to stop her sadness, by stopping her life, came back. By the time he got there she had already stopped herself. Speaking out loud, she'd told herself it was time to stop. She'd told all the hard pieces, from her first life, that they had to stop coming up in her new life. From that moment on she stopped looking at her sadness, and she soon forgot where her sadness had come from. She didn't know that she couldn't stop her sadness, not until she stopped long enough to look closely at everything that had been broken inside of her. Instead of clearing out her sadness, she drove it down deeper, hiding it where she didn't have to see it, leaving it with its need to be felt out.

After that day, she stopped looking back and was sure she was moving forward. She wouldn't look back for anything. Not even when her brother, who was still small, called and asked her to come back for him. She left the warmth of her new life to step out into the cold, and took the call of fear that wanted to pull her back. The brother, who had always gotten what he wanted, was alone and afraid of what he was about to get from some kids who were threatening him. She told him she didn't have a way to get back to help him. She told herself it was ok to turn her back on him, that he would be ok. She never came to believe that, and would feel like she'd lost her brother that night. He never sounded little again, and he started to act out big time. She never forgot that night, and never forgave herself for leaving him there on his own.

☆
## SECOND PASS AT A NEW LIFE

After the first half of this new life ended, the girl changed her life. She followed two friends from one into the next, becoming sisters with them and all their new sisters. She couldn't believe it when told she could become sisters with any house she chose since each had chosen her. She wanted to choose one of the other groups of sisters, but one of the two, the one that was her closest friend, pushed her to choose her sisters. So she let them choose her life for her. She didn't know she wasn't making her own choice, but it turned out to be a good one, even if it was their choice.

## CRISTINA COSTANTINO

At the start of this new life she thought her boy, the one that was good, was still the one for her. He came to her sister parties, and he tried to be part of her sister life, but what she liked now wasn't the life they'd shared. She saw it when she was at a party with boys who were brothers, without her boy present. At that party she saw a new boy, and she saw him in the way she had only ever seen her boy before. That night she told the new boy that he couldn't act like her boy, not while she had one. She knew what she had to do. The day after that night, she told her boy he couldn't be her boy any longer. Not if she wanted another boy like she had only ever wanted him before.

This new boy never became her boy. He would have been good to her, just as good as her first one, but the girl didn't want what was good for her. So she did a bad thing one night soon after, and she kissed one of his brothers. The boy she kissed wanted to kiss her, but he wanted to kiss a lot of girls. The girl decided she had to tell what she'd done that was bad. She didn't know telling would be bad for the boy she'd kissed. She didn't think it mattered, since she didn't think she mattered enough for it to matter.

This would be her life with boys for the rest of this life. She would keep kissing different boys that were different types of brothers. They were all good, but she would never be with one boy who was good to only her, not like when she was with her first boy from the first half of this life. That boy, whose life was too good for her, wasn't going to be in her life again. She would never get close to him again, and she'd never get that close to any other boy, not one would even come close.

The best of this part of her life were the times she had with her friends. The ones the girl called sisters, and who called her a sister in return. These friends were good, and they were good to her. A few of these friends, who were good, would be good friends past this life, until she passed them for her next new life. The life with the boy she tried to make a good life with, by leaving behind everything good that was in her life.

For now, she lived one good life with them, all of them together in a white house that shined the brightest, and kept her feeling safe behind its high wooden walls. With so many sisters around to hold her up straight, she started to walk with a straighter step. They made her look as straight as them. She couldn't make herself look that way, not on her own just yet. So the girl looked to them for help. Not much, but too much.

These good friends that had become her life had come from their own good lives, just like the good boy. Good lives, with good families, from good places. The girl could see how different she looked from them, and how much harder she had to work to look like them. Never seeing how hard some of them worked. The girl thought she had to look just like them to be liked by them. She still stood for what was good that was inside of her, that wouldn't change for anyone, but she knew it didn't have to for these friends. She may have been led to choose them, but she had chosen friends that stood for everything good, just like her. They were the same in that way, but she still chose to only show them those parts of her that were just like them, the parts that weren't broken. Since she wasn't showing anyone that, she never saw everything inside of her.

In this life, with these friends, the girl didn't have one first friend, not one like she'd had in her first life. She still had the two friends she'd followed into this life, and one of those two was still her lead good friend. She was good and good to her, but she was too big a leader to be good for her. The girl never saw how she let this friend lead her life. Since her lead friend was good it didn't lead her anywhere bad, but it would have been better for her if she had led herself her own way.

She had another friend, who never led her, who she felt led to become close to towards the end of this life. This girl, who could see the truth in people, saw the girl was more than just the half she called herself. This friend saw more of her, before she saw more of herself, and had faith in who she would become someday. During their last summer together the girl and her friend, who saw her, lived together in one room, in one apartment, with five rooms and ten of their other friends. They went to live in a big city where the girl felt everyone's energy for the first time, where she felt more of her own energy. That summer the city, with all that energy, became her city.

In that city, this friend became her friend for life, and would keep seeing her throughout her life. Their energy

## WHO BROKE THE GIRL?

matched each other and matched all the energy in the city. Running them on high, across that city, through their nights of drinking. Driving them higher, across that city, through their days of working. That summer, throughout all of this, her friend saw what she still couldn't see. The girl couldn't see why she always had to do what everyone else wanted her to, and why no one ever did what she wanted. The girl had a rant about it, and her friend asked – "What do you want to do?" She didn't know what to answer. She didn't know what she wanted.

After that summer, on the first night back that started the last year of that life, she thought she knew what she wanted. She wanted to be friends with a new girl she met while out drinking. After that night, this girl, who had hair the color of hell, would bring her hell the whole of that last year. The girl didn't know it on that night. What she thought she knew was that to be a good friend one had to be good. To be good one had to tell everything, even when everything wasn't so good.

So she told this girl that she had kissed her boy from way back when, but only after he wasn't her boy any longer. This girl from hell thought the girl wanted to hurt her, and she gave her hell that night. Then she pulled her into hell. From the first night to the last, of that entire last year, hell was behind her wherever she went. Hell gathered her group of sisters and they all pushed her around wherever she went, not leaving her a moment of happiness. The girl's hell wouldn't let her forget, so the girl never forgot. Not everyone saw the good in her.

This wouldn't be the last time the girl did the wrong thing that last year. On the last day of that life, she made a split decision to celebrate it with everyone except the family who had come to celebrate her. Without thinking about them, she kept everyone from seeing how different they were, and from seeing how different she was from everyone. Only, everyone saw it anyways. She was the only one with no one there to celebrate her.

She didn't tell her family the truth when she saw them later that day, knowing her truth wasn't a good one. She told them she couldn't find them after the big celebration, where they had sat surrounded by the families of strangers. She told them she had looked, and never told them about the smaller celebration where she was with the families of her friends, the ones that were strangers to her. The family that everyone thought never understood what was said understood everything. That day the girl's shame, from everything bad, kept her from doing what would have been good. She never forgot the added shame of what she'd done that day.

☆
## WHEN HER PAST CHANGED

Before the girl moved back to the big city where she wanted to start her next life, she spent some time back in her first life. She needed to go back to make enough to kick off her new start. She went to live in the house that had stopped feeling cold, sat on the road that wasn't the only one she knew now. Living with the family that didn't want to stop her from having fun. The girl didn't stay long, just long enough to find more of the good in that life.

For a time, she found a friend in her first friend again. Before she went off to start her next new life, they enjoyed this time together. While with her, she became close with two of her close friends. These four close friends laughed together, ate together, drank together, dressed up together and danced together. The girl found a lot of happiness and forgot more of her sadness while revisiting this life. She thought she had lost all the weight from this life, but what was still hidden inside wouldn't let itself stay forgotten for much longer.

The guy, who was her good friend, was still being good to her, even though the girl wouldn't let him be as good as he wanted. She felt pressured by him when she felt how much she mattered to him. So she put distance between herself and this guy who always put her first. She chose to put herself closer to her first friend, who still put her second. Instead of sticking to her, this guy found what he needed with someone who wanted him. He'd understood he wouldn't be with her, and then she understood she'd lost him as a friend. He couldn't do what was good for him while being good to her first.

The girl settled into this life briefly, but the voice inside of her wouldn't let her settle into it for long. This was only meant to be a moment of rest. There was more she had to do and this couldn't come close to being it for her. There were more places she had to live, more people she had to meet, and more things she had to do. Settling there would do nothing but hold her back from all of that. The voice knew this wasn't supposed to be her life for much longer. She had to move so she could see more, to understand more about herself.

## WHO BROKE THE GIRL?

The time came to move to the city where she'd felt so much energy. Where her friends, who had once been her sisters, had already moved their energy. She turned to her lead friend, the one that had helped her first find those sisters, and asked her for help finding the first place she would work. Her help worked, and the girl found work that she felt would make her happy. She would help make little stories, made for little eyes, look beautiful while being read to them. The girl loved the idea of imagining up what these little stories would look like for all the little ones who were going to love them.

But before she could leave the family that wasn't as sad anymore, for the new life she was imagining, they were hit with the sadness of sickness. The mother, who'd made herself strong, was weakened. The body that had made each of them turned on her, which made them all suffer. The part of her that had fed them when they were first born was eating away at her. They all cried out in pain, but none more than her father. This man who'd made her afraid, was afraid. This man who'd yelled, would never yell again. The fear of losing her mother killed all of her father's anger.

The family heard quickly that her sickness didn't run deep, and that this hard time would only last a short time, so they didn't let the girl stop her time. The family that had modeled how much work mattered, said her new work mattered more than sitting with her mother. The girl should have stayed, but instead of making her stay, they pushed her to go. So she went off to build the life she couldn't wait to get to. The girl learned this last lesson before she moved away from them. She learned to put work over what mattered in life.

☆
## A NEW LIFE WITH OLD ENERGY

This time, when the girl moved out, she was able to push herself further. Soon enough she would go even farther, until the day would come when she kept going farther and farther. With every move she thought she was moving away from her past, never realizing her past was moving with her. For now, she only wanted to go back to the city with all of her energy and all of her friends. She moved to the city life she already knew, but it was a new life for her.

She went to the city that had already become hers, thinking she would never leave it again. She never imagined she'd come to move away, only to come back time and again. This time, her friend who could see her helped her find her way into her new life. She would live with her when she first got there, and then live in two other places. She'd move between these three places in half as many years, but would only work in that one place that was everything she imagined it would be. She would only make one friend, from there, into a close friend who would stay grounded in her life for decades. She would only make one boy matter, but before she met him, she started making herself matter.

The place where the girl worked to create stories had words from all the stories on the floor, across every floor. She loved walking these floors, she loved all of the stories she worked on, and she loved all of the women she worked with. Each of them looked different, but was the same in one way. All were strong women. The girl saw the strength in these women each day, and she decided to be just like them. The girl found her strength at work, not knowing someday she would give all of her strength away to her work. By the time she saw that she would have to leave her work behind, to find her real strength.

For now the girl loved to work. She didn't make a lot at this work, but she made enough. Enough to have good times with her friends in this life, the same ones she'd spent all of her time with in her last life. Everyone she knew was the same as they had been before, except they had stopped calling each other sisters. They all lived in different spaces in this city they shared, and they were all trying to find their own space. So even though the spent time together, the space between them started to grow, now that they weren't sharing a life like before.

The girl had enough space to split her life between her old friends, her grounded friend and her first friend from her first life. She went back often to visit her and the mother who was getting better. Her first friend came to the city, but she didn't come to visit the girl. She came with one sister to visit their other sister, the one who now lived in the same city as the girl. Whenever they came the girl left her space behind to squeeze into their space. She'd spend those times with them like they were her family, wandering her city like she was visiting it with them. Head-to-toe, the four would squeeze into sleep together, as if they were all sisters. She was happy to be packed in so tight, feeling the weight of them beside her.

The girl was happy in this life, and she was happy when she went back to visit her first life. That's where she found the boy who she was going to make matter. The girl had never seen him before, but she saw something she liked in him that first time she saw him. She couldn't see how much he'd been broken, by the hard life he'd grown up in, until it was too late for her. By then all she saw was how much she wanted to help him, and couldn't see where this need came from. If she had known all the good she would leave behind for him, she would have left him to be broken, and gone off to help herself. The girl couldn't see what was good for her. She only saw what was good for him. He had never had a good life, and she wanted him to have one, so she gave him hers.

Even before the girl gave her whole life over, he took her over. She could have seen it, but the girl had already learned how to look past the bad, to see the good. She couldn't see how he controlled her. Even though she saw his control at dinner, during a visit to her city. The dinner where his hand stopped hers, to stop her from eating what he said wasn't good for her. She couldn't see that he needed more attention than anyone should need. Even though she saw him move her over so he could get more from others, after he had already taken everything she gave him. She couldn't see how much he was hiding. Even though she saw herself look the other way every time she heard him lie to anyone, about anything. She couldn't see the anger that threatened to come up from inside of him. Even though she saw herself quiet down every time it started to threaten her.

She wouldn't look at everything shouting at her to run from what was already too broken. She only cared about how much he made her laugh, when she wasn't cringing, more than any boy she had ever met before him. She could only see how much he needed her, and how much she needed that. She could only feel how much she was starting to feel for this broken boy. She only knew she liked the weight of him, that felt so familiar, when he pressed it all down on her, covering all of her with all of him, in their broken way of hugging.

## WHO BROKE THE GIRL?

The girl, who was just starting to make her own choices, made the choice to stop making any good choices for herself. The girl, who was starting to get attention for herself first, let herself be moved back to second. The girl, who didn't have to feel fear anymore, went back to loving full of fear. The girl, who was starting to get what she had always wanted, couldn't see that this life she was choosing was the life she had already had, the life she had never wanted.

The first friend saw this broken boy when the girl first saw him, and she saw him hurt the girl every time she came back to see them. She never saw how much more he would hurt her after he moved to her city for her. By then their friendship had been broken. On another night that the boy made the girl sad, he made the first friend mad. The girl's tears made her first friend yell, and that made the girl mad. They turned on each other, and then they turned away from each other. The girl wouldn't be told that she shouldn't feel sad. She could only stop being sad when she was ready to make herself happy.

Instead of finding her happiness, she moved sadness closer. She brought this broken boy back to her city with her, with the promise to move to a city he chose if he didn't like the one she'd chosen. Her old friends in this new life knew this broken boy wasn't good enough to her, and they knew he wasn't good enough for her. The family, that had once made her sad, knew this boy could only make her sad. No one told her what to do, but the time came when she knew what she had to do. The things he did to make her sad were taking over all the time they shared that should have been happy. She didn't want to be this sad, and the voice inside of her pushed her to push him out. She pushed him, but she didn't push herself hard enough. She made the choice that was good for her, then after a short time she changed her choice. She chose to go back to him, and she gave back her good life.

Everyone knew the girl wanted him, so everyone accepted when she moved her life in with him. No one knew what the girl didn't know. She needed to help him by giving him a good life, because of the broken girl inside of her, the one she didn't know how to help. No one knew what the girl knew but couldn't face. No one in his life would ever accept her. Not because of her, but because of him. He was too broken to tell anyone in his life that she mattered to him. He hid her from all of them. Afraid to give her any of their attention, and take away from the attention they gave him that he needed so much.

Then came the choice that would move her even further in the wrong direction, and closer to the sadness she still had to see to clear. It would change this life, and change the direction her life would take. She chose to move herself away from what could have been a good life, in a good city, with good friends. She made the choice to move herself farther away. The girl turned her good road down, with one big push, by keeping the promise he wasn't pushing her to keep. She chose to move their energy away

## WHO BROKE THE GIRL?

from her city, full of good energy for her, to a city south of there. To run down a new life that they could start together, where she thought he wouldn't be able to keep her hidden.

WHO BROKE THE GIRL?

☆
## ROUND ONE IN THE WARM CITY

The girl drove away from her city through the darkest night, following the broken boy as he drove his small truck. She drove the big, broken truck loaded with all of their stuff, down a road being hit by a hard, breaking rain. Now the broken boy was pushing. Driving her to drive faster than the loaded truck could manage, she moved away from her city faster than she should. She stood the whole way on one leg to push her foot down harder, but she couldn't drive the broken truck fast enough for him. Pushing to get them to a city where they still hadn't found work. A city that still hadn't found out how much work it took to be them. He only stopped them long enough to show her his anger, the anger that threatened to push her straight off their road that night. A road already breaking under the weight of their new life.

At the end of that road they saw that their new city was full of roads. Ones that looked new to them, but were the same old roads that had been around since way back when. Roads lined with trees too old to be moved for anything new that wanted to come in. Old trees with branches that arched across their roads, spaced too close to let any light touch the ground the couple drove on. Every road was a long one, and they circled their new city with its new buildings that were shadowed by old trees. The roads changed their names, with no sign of reason, to become different roads straight out of nowhere. The couple drove in circles that first year of their new life. Learning their way down one road, only to find themselves on a new road once it changed unexpectedly on them.

The couple circled around the same fight that first year of their new life. In each he would say nothing, which told her everything. A silent stare was returned when she said he was making her sad. The girl wasn't listening to what she should have heard. He was showing her know how much sadder he was going to make her. A part of her knew she shouldn't push forward with this broken life she'd pushed for. A life with this boy who wouldn't kiss her, wouldn't hold her, and couldn't love her; except in his own broken way.

## WHO BROKE THE GIRL?

They still used all of their weight to press each other down, but now the girl could feel herself straining to lighten up.

She called her old friends, and she called out what she knew was broken in her new life. They were still good enough friends to listen. Then the girl made another call, a bad one that would hurt a good friend who had been good to her. She called this friend to say she couldn't go back to her good life for one day, to celebrate her wedding day. The boy didn't say he didn't want to go, but the girl could feel in the air between them how much he didn't want to spend the money. She had to stop the tension before it turned on her, even though it might never have made that turn.

The girl couldn't see how bad this call was that she was making, that she had started to make when she started down this road with that first choice that was leading her to nothing but sadness. Her call made her good friend mad enough to break away from her. The girl felt her guilt, and stopped calling all the friends they shared, including the one who had always been able to see her. She couldn't bring herself to see how that one might see her now. She didn't try to replace any of them by making any good friends in her new city. She couldn't while spaced too close to the broken boy to let any light into her life.

The couple with one car, no work, and no friends learned to spend all of their time together. With no space between them, and so much space from anyone they knew, they grew closer together. They grew too tight to grow. The girl was the second of two again, and she found the safety she recognized there. While they stuck to each other she could only keep her balance, with the boy whose broken pieces tripped her up, by leaning on him. So she leaned on him too much, and started to lean over.

The space between her and her good friends was too wide for her to reach out to them, but the space to reach her family was manageable. It took too many hours to go back to see them too often, but she still went back. The father who'd stopped yelling, had gotten gentler. He only spoke words about how much he loved her, even though he didn't really know her. The mother who'd been weakened, had grown stronger. She only spoke words she thought would help her in life, even though she didn't really understand her life. The space between them was small, but the space she kept from her sister and brother was as wide as ever. She couldn't cross that space and face what she could see, in their lives, that had been broken by their past. She would go back with the boy to see her broken family, who could never understand why she was with this broken boy.

In this life the boy made one good friend that shared his space at work. He was a good guy. He was a good friend to the broken boy, and he wanted to be a good friend to her. When together, this guy always asked the same good question. With a laugh, he would ask, what the hell a girl like her was doing with a boy like that. The girl heard his laugh, but could see that his eyes were asking a serious question.

## WHO BROKE THE GIRL?

She always came back with what she thought she knew, and told him that the broken boy was good. This guy was good enough to know better. He knew nothing good would come down the road with this broken boy, and soon enough he walked away from what was so broken.

The broken boy, who never understood why this guy walked out, walked himself away from where they worked. The girl understood. Only someone like her, who had already lived through so much that was broken, could stay so close to someone so broken. This good guy couldn't really see her. He couldn't see the broken pieces inside of her that she kept hidden. She wasn't as broken as the boy, but she was broken enough to be with him. She understood something else that didn't matter enough to her. To the good guy, she had mattered. The good guy left the life he questioned, and the girl stayed with the answer she never questioned.

The girl wouldn't question her life with the boy for a while, but she questioned herself, at her new work, every day. When they moved down there she'd left behind the work she loved. She still worked on stories, but now she worked to create stories that sold people happy dreams. She questioned herself every day she did that that first year. Questioning if she liked creating this work, and questioning if she was good enough to do it, she questioned herself straight out of creating and straight into selling. She started selling people who created, to people who needed something created. She loved those people who created, and she hated selling them.

WHO BROKE THE GIRL?

☆
## ROUND TWO IN THE WARM CITY

In the second year of their new life the boy's new work brought them new friends. He saw these friends at work every day, and these friends saw the good that she saw in him. He didn't hide her from them, but then again he didn't have to. She was so different from them that they couldn't really see her and didn't bother looking at her all that much, so they didn't give any of his attention away to her. They loved giving all of their attention to the broken boy, especially since he put on a good show every time they were with them. She stayed quiet most of the hours they spent in that group, especially during those shows that were too loud for her. Hour after hour was spent with these friends. Hours everyone considered as happy, hours where she worked hard to look happy.

There was one girl in this group that enjoyed the boy's shows but wanted to give her just as much attention as she gave him. She had a really big heart this one, and she had her own boy she held love for in that heart. He was another good guy who wanted to be a good guy friend to the broken boy. So the four became couples that were good friends. They weren't the only couples. Everyone in their new group was part of a couple, and everyone came to everything as a couple.

After making friends with them the broken boy started making a new move. He pushed the girl to be like all the other couples and buy a home as one. The voice inside of her pushed against this move. The girl pushed the boy back a little, but only for a little while, then she got herself ready to move. She decided she wanted this move that was too early for her and it became their choice made by him. She gave in even though they didn't have any money to put down, and he didn't have the credit to cover anything. Her family gave them what they needed so she could get them the home he wanted. She paid the price up front, and she would pay an even bigger price later.

On the day of the closing she noticed the boy didn't have a line to sign on their contract. She looked at all the older men, staring at her from around the table, to find out why hers was the only name they wanted. These men

## WHO BROKE THE GIRL?

misunderstood her, so they explained that the broken boy's bad credit wouldn't let him claim any of the debt for their home. She had come in knowing that. She wanted to know why the men had kept the boy off the papers deeding their home to them. Without question, she wanted to take the debt on as her own and share the claim together. Shocked, they asked her – "Why would you ever do that?" The men told her not to, but she did. The girl didn't know how to do what was good for her, even when she was told the right thing to do.

This wrong move felt right for a time. Life seemed to change for the broken couple in their new home. The boy changed. He had the good life the girl had wanted to give him, and he seemed happy in it. She thought they were both happy in this life where they did everything together. Cooking their dinners together. Painting their home together. Working out at their gym together. Shopping for their clothes together. Taking walks and runs through their neighborhood together. All of their time together changed the girl. She stopped asking for anything and took the love the boy gave when he gave it, in whatever way he chose to give it. She chose to believe it was enough for her. Now that she stopped fighting for more, the fight they'd fought stopped its screams against this life.

Work changed for the girl after they were in their new home. She couldn't bring herself to keep selling instead of creating so she left the work she didn't believe in. She didn't go back to being one of those who created, she went back to a place that created and helped protect the work they created that sold people happiness. They made beautiful work that told beautiful stories. The owner, who was the lead creative, treated her like a partner. She created the space for everyone to create by taking the hits of anger, meant for the whole team, from the people who paid for their work. The girl would take in their anger until it grew quiet. Then she'd take their apology, and at times the flowers it came with. Always knowing that neither meant the anger would stop coming. In this new place that she loved, she may not have been the one creating but she found space for herself in their work. Using her mind, she would think out upfront how to make their work smarter while working alongside the lead creative. The girl was happy doing all that she could to get beautiful work out into the world.

These events that changed much of their life didn't go deep enough. Life in this house seemed good on the surface, but what was inside of him was still simmering, waiting to pull everything out from under her. The girl had gotten good at looking the other way whenever his tension bubbled, but soon it would be out in the open so often that there'd be nowhere else to look. His tension was thrown at her the morning she felt happiness at her sister's news that she was having her first boy. Her happiness pushed her to hurry up and tell the broken boy, but she pushed too hard, and when her move knocked against his cup, some of the coffee he loved drinking sloshed over. Anger tensed up his face and filled the air between them, pushing her to quickly move away from him. Her happiness had spilled his, and she knew better.

Despite these moments of tension that were rising, she started to look happier when she was with their group of couple friends. She had forgotten enough of what used to make her happy to be able to enjoy them. During all the hours they drank through after work and all the parties they drank at, in all the couples' homes, at the end of every week. They drank a lot with all these friends who couldn't see how the boy could look. They could only see how much the boy could make them laugh. They never saw how much the boy needed to make them laugh. The girl didn't think she needed anyone except the boy to see her. Not until the boy met this other girl at work. A girl he started wanting to see more than he wanted to see her.

CRISTINA COSTANTINO

WHO BROKE THE GIRL?

## LEFT ALONE TO A SLOW DEATH

The girl was wise, even though she hadn't made very many wise choices. She tried to do what she thought was wise about this other girl, and she chose to understand why the boy needed to spend so much time with her. She knew he could have his own friend, even if it was a girl who didn't want to be friends with her. She didn't want to make it hard for the boy to be friends with this other girl, even though the way they went about it would have been hard for anyone to handle. The girl tried hard to pretend it wasn't hard for her. Then they decided to make it harder for her to make pretend.

CRISTINA COSTANTINO

    This other girl now went to all the happy hours with all the other couples. Happy hours the boy told the girl not to come to. Hours that ran into the late hours, night after night. Never with her, and never telling her when these hours would start or when they would end. They never talked about what happened during these hours that the girl used to share with him as half of one of the couples at them. She wanted to give him the space she could see he needed so she stopped asking to go with him. She only asked him to give her a few hours a week, but he didn't have enough to give her any. Even when the boy spent a few of his hours at home with her, there wasn't any peace for her. Late night calls from this other girl constantly broke through the girl's time with him.

    Then a time came that the couple went away for two nights to celebrate when they had first become a couple, four years earlier. They had a good first day, followed by an early night. Then the girl woke up late at night, alone in a bed that was empty. She found the boy outside, on a call with this other girl. She waited, silently, for their call to end, and then she asked him, quietly, why there had to be a call in the middle of the night, in the middle of their weekend. The boy looked at her and stayed silent. The girl couldn't bring herself to speak or smile for the rest of that weekend.

    Then it got harder for her to stay silent. The girl, who had never looked through his things, picked up, to move over, what the boy had put down at night and forgotten to pick up on his way out in the morning. Her hand didn't try to feel what it felt, and her heart couldn't stand how it felt. She felt the crumbled up shell of what he had used for protection, and despite everything, wasn't prepared to protect her heart from this. The pain pierced straight through. She couldn't look at the truth in her hand, and she couldn't stand under the weight of this much pain. She crumbled. So when the boy told her a story about the joke that had led it to be in his pocket, she didn't look at it closely. The story that she knew, inside of her, was made up to make her stay with him.

The girl tried hard to be ok with this and all the stories he kept spinning. She tried to be ok with the boy going out with this other girl more than he stayed in with her. She tried to be ok with the boy talking to this other girl more than he talked to her. She tried to be ok by herself when she was alone in their home, so much. She tried to be ok with the boy when he was in their home, so little. She tried to be ok by making friends of her own that she could get out of their home with. She tried to be ok in this new life she was now living. The girl wasn't ok.

She felt how he didn't want to live their life together anymore, and she couldn't stop the pain from sobbing up out of her. Feeling so alone when she was in their home alone, she couldn't stand to be there. Sleepless, while alone, she drove those long roads at night, circling the city with all of her hard thoughts about this life that was changing on her. Those thoughts drained her. Forgetting to eat when alone, she'd force down a bite after a few days of not having taken one so she could continue to function. There wasn't a moment of respite. She'd curl up on the cold bathroom floor at work when left there alone. Sobbing for the life she couldn't stop from losing.

The girl tried to shrink away from the pain inside of her, and she shrank in the world around her. The girl, who had never wanted to take up too much space, was taking up less space. Her head, that was full of too many sad thoughts, looked bigger and dropped lower between shoulders that had grown sharper. She couldn't help but show everyone her bones as she shrank to less than a zero. She stood on legs that didn't have the strength left to hold her up and couldn't fill the pants she'd been wearing. Legs that couldn't move her out of the way fast enough to miss the next hard kick from the broken boy. The final kick that once delivered would knock what was left out of her.

The girl never yelled for the boy to stop what he was doing. She asked questions to try to understand why he was doing it. She asked him if he still wanted to be with her. He did. She asked him if this other girl was who his soul wanted him to be with. He didn't know. She asked him to let her go if he couldn't be good to her. He stayed silent. She knew he wouldn't. He wanted them both. She never asked herself why she was letting him get away with what he was doing. She never asked herself why she wouldn't let him go.

The broken boy never did give the girl a reason for what he was doing. She suffered through thinking he didn't want her anymore, until she could come to accept that,

## WHO BROKE THE GIRL?

without understanding that the life they had made scared him. The boy, who had only ever known a broken life, couldn't lose a good one. So he kept pushing away what scared him until he broke their life. He kept pushing away the girl until he broke her, before she could break him, more than he was already broken.

Soon, another time came to go away, one that would give the girl another hard push. While away a call came while the boy was in the shower. The girl, who never looked through his phone, looked over at his phone. She saw this other girl was calling, and she finally saw what she hadn't been able to see until then. She had zero power over her own happiness. The girl had given the boy everything she had to give, and he had thrown everything away. He had all the power, and he didn't care about her happiness. He never had and never would. The girl was struck silent by this sight. When the time came to go back home, he drove them, and she didn't speak for hours. The girl had seen too much to go back.

When they got to their road she closed the door behind her and went into their home. The boy turned the car around to go down a different road. The girl knew that's what he would do and it was what she wanted. Alone in their home, she took back some of her power. Taking out a pen, she wrote down what she couldn't speak, letting out the words that let go of him. She left the boy alone in the home she'd bought for him, leaving him to this other girl, the one he now wanted.

CRISTINA COSTANTINO

WHO BROKE THE GIRL?

## **BREAKING OUT OF A BROKEN LIFE**

The girl made a good choice in leaving, even though she no longer had her own home to live in. She now slept in between the two homes of the two new friends she'd made. They were good to her, and they cared enough to listen to her, as much as she needed. The group of couples wouldn't talk to her. They could only blame her, but she had never wanted to talk to them before and didn't care to now. The only ones who spoke to her were the couple with the big heart. The break made their heart ache, but they didn't blame her, and they wanted to keep her as a friend. The girl, who still felt loyal, kept quiet to these two about how the broken boy had broken them. She still spoke to them but less than her new friends, the ones she could speak to about everything.

The girl's sadness had started to quiet down. The pain that sobbed out of her before wasn't sobbing up anymore. She thought she was pushing all the sadness out with all of her power. She wasn't happy yet, not really, but she felt how she could make herself happy now. The girl could smile with her new friends, and she always went out with one of them. The girl talked to some new boys, and she started to go out with one of them. The girl wanted it to be her time to be happy. She had let the broken boy go so they could both be happy now. She didn't know that he wasn't ready to let her go off and be happy.

The couple that had broken up met to break apart the pieces of their couple life. To break her off their home and his car, that she had taken the debt for with her name. To break his car off her papers, that gave it her protection. To break their one account apart into two single ones. The girl went without knowing that the boy wasn't ready to break apart his life. He would only try to break her that day. They spoke and broke nothing. Then she told him, kindly, she would never forget what had been good between them and could never hate him. Without hesitation, he replied hatefully – "I fucked this other girl." Her heart stopped and her hands covered her face. His heart laughed, and his face smiled. Then he told her – "I'm just kidding. I wanted to make you say I hate you."

## WHO BROKE THE GIRL?

The girl left without saying those words or any others. She went back to the life where she was trying to be happy, even though she was still living in-between other people's lives. She didn't know how to break off the pieces of her old life, and she didn't know that the broken boy wasn't done trying to break her. The girl met him again on another night he asked to see her. She didn't want to go, but he pushed her hard, and she didn't have enough power to push him away, to keep pushing for herself.

She still felt her loyalty to the choice she had made to have a life with him, and she didn't know how to let go of that promise. She knew too well how to work too hard to keep a broken life together. The boy worked hard to turn their night into a weekend, and she let it work. Just one weekend together, in the home that was no longer theirs. They spent it pretending they were still a couple. Two days spent driving all the roads they had once driven when they first moved there. Looking at the big homes, full of happy lives, that they had once spoken about having. Nights spent together, with no calls to interrupt them, before they went to sleep next to each other. The girl set her sadness aside, and she let herself forget that sadness wouldn't let itself be forgotten. The first day of the week, after that weekend, their time to pretend came to its end. That morning, he told her that she could sleep in their home's second room that night.

Later that day the boy called to tell her he wouldn't see her until later that night. Only, the boy wasn't seeing who the girl was becoming. She wasn't the same girl that had slept next to him before, and she wasn't going to sleep through what he was doing, not like she had before. That night the girl went to see for herself, she went where he said he would be with some other boy. The girl knew what she would see, now that she was looking, and it was exactly what she saw. She sat herself down with the boy, this other girl, and the bottle of wine between them. She looked at them, with a quiet sadness, and she asked – "Do you care that you're killing me?"

They stayed silent in the face of her sadness, and then turned their backs to walk away from her. The girl, who didn't want to stay silent any longer, followed this other girl. She asked her quiet question one more time. This other girl looked at her with her small, hard eyes. Then the boy called, and she only had to say – "She's here." The phone was handed to her, and the boy told the girl, with his quiet coldness – "Get away from her." She moved herself away, but she couldn't get away from the boy who would go even further to break her.

Before too long he came back to the girl to ask her to kindly come back to him for longer than one weekend. The girl knew she didn't want to go back. He told her everything would be different. The girl knew nothing would be different. He told her he wanted their old life back, before this other girl had come into it. The girl knew she wanted the new life she was starting, with her new friends and a new boy she had met. Only, she still didn't know how to break

## WHO BROKE THE GIRL?

off from this old life. Her new life was still too in-between both lives, too in-between other people's homes, for her to hold on to. So she broke off her new life and went back to him, but she couldn't go back and live.

Their life back together lasted longer than one weekend, but it didn't last much longer than that. The girl couldn't forget everything the boy had done and all the pain she had felt was still hurting. The voice inside of her pushed her to speak out. The girl, who still wouldn't yell, couldn't stop speaking. Not even that one time, and then the next, he used his hands to threaten her, to stop her from speaking the feelings he didn't want to hear. He pressed them against her throat when she wouldn't stop pressing him with her words. Pressing her back against a wall, he trapped her, but she couldn't stay trapped in this broken life much longer.

One afternoon, after nothing had happened and nothing had changed, the girl broke her promise to live this broken life she had never wanted. She had suffered like this, for this life, month-after-month for seven months. She couldn't escape this sadness while living with him, and she couldn't live with this sadness any longer. She was done now. She told him they were really done now. She told him he was going to have to move out of her house now. The boy responded with silence, then he left the house, only to come back in the early hours. The girl heard him outside, and she knew what she was hearing. She went out to see the boy on another one of his calls with this other girl. She broke now.

The girl, who knew a yell wouldn't change anything, started yelling. Yell after yell from outside to in, downstairs to up, and back and-forth from their room to the second. The girl's yells kept growing louder. The boy told her to stop, but she couldn't stop herself. So he stopped her. He gave her a hard slap of his anger, from the back of his hand to the side of her face. The slap, harder than any slap of fear she had ever felt, made her feel more fear than she had ever felt. The tears of pain, from the months of torment, started sobbing out of her.

She tried backing herself away from what was hurting her, and she backed herself against a wall. The broken boy followed her back. His hands circling her throat, his lips to her ear, his threat got louder. He whispered – "If you don't stop crying I'll kill you." The girl knew he could. She struggled, fearing she couldn't make herself stay quiet now. Finally finding the strength to stop, she never found out if he would have done what she knew he could. Everything stopped now.

The boy took his time leaving her house. Not a lot, but more than enough. She told him to sleep in the room that had been theirs since she didn't want to sleep there now. She slept in the second room, where he had once tried to send her and then threatened her. The one she didn't have a way to keep him from entering. Over and over she woke up in the late hours, the ones she'd gotten used to being alone in. She wasn't alone now. The broken boy would sit in the dark with his back to the door, watching her with a broken look. He didn't look like he wanted to break her now. He said her he didn't want to lose her now. Over and over he asked her to give him another chance. She kept repeating – "You already lost me."

WHO BROKE THE GIRL?

☆
## MAKING THE LAST BREAK

The girl was stronger, and the boy was weakened by her strength. She had no love left for him, but she felt bad for him, even though the boy had never felt for her when he was hurting her. She listened when this sad, broken boy needed to talk to her. She listened when he needed to cry to her. She listened when he needed to tell her his life would end without her. No matter how many kind words she offered him, his sadness wouldn't stop, then it started to turn on her so the girl decided it was time to stop listening.

She stopped when the angry, broken boy tried to make her feel guilty by saying he'd seen her out with another boy. She stopped when he yelled he would pound her head in for not picking up when he called her. She stopped when he threatened to burn her house down before he'd sign it over to her. Month-after-month, for twelve months after the girl let the boy go, he tried to hold on to her. First with his sadness over losing her, then with his anger at her leaving him. He refused to let go of her.

The broken boy's words threatened the girl, but he couldn't hurt her, not like he had before. Still, the father who used to scare her was scared for her. She'd told him pieces of what had happened. Not a lot, but enough for him to try to help her in the only way he knew how. Her father called the broken boy and threatened to break him in two if he didn't stop calling her. Instead of stopping, the boy called her with a new threat. He would call the police on her father if he ever called him again. Afraid for him, she told her father that he had to stop. She knew she could only help herself.

The boy may have stopped living in her house, but he kept his control over her through the house she had put him on. He refused to take his name off her house. He told her she had to give him money, more than he had ever put into the house, and more than anyone would pay for it. She would have, but she didn't have it to give him. He refused to move his mail to his new house. He made her personally hand him what was still coming to her house. He refused to give her his keys, and he told her he'd call the police if she changed the locks to her house. One night the girl came home after going out with a new boy to find the broken boy

## WHO BROKE THE GIRL?

waiting for her in her house. That's when she decided it was time to move out and let strangers live in the house that was keeping her trapped to him.

The friends she had once pretended were hers still had no words for her, which was still fine by her. But a friend from his past, a girl, wouldn't stop emailing words over to her. This friend, who had never had a word to say to her before, tried to convince the girl to go back to the broken boy. The girl sent back kind words, trying to be helpful, but she stayed strong. She wasn't going back to a broken past. Then this girl wrote words that blamed her for when the boy's hands had hurt her. She told the girl she had better not tell anyone these words that weren't true. The girl couldn't believe this threat. To protect the boy, she hadn't told anyone these words that were true. She felt attacked for having been attacked. She told this friend of his to never send her another word. She didn't want to think about the past for one minute longer.

The girl eventually found a way to stop the boy. She used the way of being that he had shown her. She threatened him. Her way out came in the mail he had once used to control her. A letter came that said his name had been added to her card, and he could use her credit with full approval. At first, she forgot she had chosen to add him back when they still shared a life. Instead, she remembered he had enough of her information to have done it since she'd once given him all of it to open a fund for her through his work. She remembered the truth, but it didn't stop her from doing what she knew she had to. Something that was wrong by him but right for her. She called and threatened to call his work and tell them he'd stolen her information from his computer at work. She knew what she threatened to do would kill him at work, and she didn't want to hurt him, but she wanted to kill the control he wielded over her. When she made the threat she heard the shock in his voice as he told her how much this could hurt him. Coldly, she replied – "I know, and I never want to hear from you again. Or else I will." He heard her, and she never heard from him again. She had taken back control of her life.

WHO BROKE THE GIRL?

☆
## FROM BUILDING BACK TO BREAKING

Even while the broken boy was pushing his sadness and anger on her, she was working on building her happiness. She was making a hard push to get a good life back and that's when she made a hard, but good call. She called the old friend from her old life, the one who had always been able to see her. This friend, who she hadn't spoken to in years, told her she had been waiting for this call for years. She had known the girl well enough to know she would know her again one day. They told each other all about the lives they'd lived apart, and even though they still lived in different parts of the country, they would never part from each other's lives again.

In this new life the girl was building in the warm city, she was living in a new house with one of her new friends. One whose house she had stayed in when she was living in-between homes. This new friend felt just like the first friend from her first life. Just like that friend then, the girl needed this friend to walk alongside her. The girl, who didn't want to be alone anymore, made this friend the second friend who was always with her. She could see how alike they were, both good women who led their own lives, and she wanted to be more like that and nothing like the girl she'd been when with the broken boy. She liked how both of them had lived the same number of years and had both come down from up north. They both did the same work, selling people happiness, and after work they went out to find boys they could have a good time with. The two grew close doing all the same things, all the time.

When they went out there were always a lot of boys around them, and they each went out with a few of them. Then they made friends with a lot of them. They became good friends with one big group of boys that had been good friends since they were little boys. A few of these boys lived together in one house where the door was always open to everyone. These would be the boys who helped her forget the broken boy. Boys she surrounded herself with during the day and at night. She never had to feel alone with all these boys around her.

## WHO BROKE THE GIRL?

The warm city, circled by all the roads she had once driven down at night, became a new city for her. Now her nights were full of drinks, drunk while laughing. She had her group of boys that she loved, that could love her back. A group of boys she filled her life with by doing everything in her life with them. They cooked family-style dinners together, watched movies together, worked out together, drove to the beach together, and played tough games together. A group of boys she could be just like a boy with. The girl made herself matter by making herself matter to them.

These were her core boys, but there were others, ones the girl wanted to go out with alone. She went out with a lot, but she always kept an eye out for the one boy who she had liked first. The boy she'd gone out with when she left the broken boy that first time. They saw each other while out, and the two would go out together every so often. This boy had liked the girl when he'd first seen her, but then he saw what the girl couldn't see. She looked like the happiest girl having more fun than anyone around her, but she was just a sad girl having a lot of fun. Her sadness was being carried around inside while the outside was smiling. He knew she was still too sad for the two of them to be happy together. He would try her out, every so often, but it was always too soon for them to work out. Her sadness finally bubbled up one night when he'd promised to come for her, but never came. She cried out in a message, asking him why he was always hurting her. That message, sent to the wrong boy, killed off anything that might have been between them.

The girl, who thought she was only carrying around her happiness, was happiest when she was being carried. Her group of boys thought she was happy, and they were more than happy to carry her on their backs. At times the girl, who thought she was strong enough, carried one of her boys on her back, no matter how much bigger than her they were. At night after drinking, and during the day before drinking, everyone in her group picked the girl up and carried her everywhere.

Through all of this, the girl, who was carrying less of the weight from her broken past, stayed friends with the couple that had the really big heart. Not as much as before, but enough for the girl with the big heart to ask her to be one of the ones standing next to her on the day she became a wife. She didn't want to, but she couldn't say no so she said yes. The broken boy was asked and said no. He wouldn't stand up, and he wouldn't go anywhere near them that day, not with the girl standing there.

That day, the girl stood up and faced all his friends from their broken past. All the ones that wouldn't talk to her looked at her, and she felt them judge her. The girl drank more than she could to stay as long as she should. Then she ran from those hard faces to meet the faces of the friends she thought could see her. That's when the girl broke her face. A new friend, one with long skinny legs, saw she was in pain so she tried to lift her up. The girl tried to jump up onto

## WHO BROKE THE GIRL?

her back, but those skinny legs couldn't stay up under her weight. They were on a road that sloped down, and before she could make it all the way up, they both went straight down. With her hands trapped behind a skinny back, the girl hit the hard road face first.

Her second friend ran back. She saw her friends had fallen, but she didn't know which one needed her. The skinny friend was crying. The girl was laughing. Then the girl saw her second friend's face drop when they came face-to-face. The girl's tongue touched the jagged edges inside of her, and her hands touched the blood running down her. She stopped laughing and started running. When she got home she faced a mirror and thought – "I'll never look good again." Five teeth broken in half, two lips torn in two, one chin and two shoulders ripped to shreds. She could see how much was broken and her pain sobbed out, as loud as it had ever sobbed before.

The second friend came and told her she had to stop crying out so loudly. The skinny friend, who had chipped one tooth, felt guilty and shouldn't have to hear the girl's pain. The skinny friend, who couldn't hear the girl, went home. The second friend, who couldn't help the girl, decided to go back out. The girl was being left alone with her pain. She didn't get mad, but she felt hurt. The second friend got mad at her for being hurt. She yelled at her that she couldn't always be with her; she had other friends who needed her. The girl didn't say a word, she understood in that moment that they had been together too much, and her friend needed a break. But that night she had needed her friend to stay with her and would never forgive her for leaving her alone when she was in pain. The girl broke off their friendship after the night she broke her face.

The girl didn't ask anyone for help that night or the next day. She went to find help the first day of the week. The first man she asked for help, a doctor, looked at her with contempt. He asked her – "What did you do to yourself?" Then he told her – "You'll carry your scars for life." The girl sat in his chair and silently cried, feeling all the pain inside of her. Then she left and found a second man, a doctor who wanted to help her. He was kind to her that day and all the days she had to go back for more help. When he was done helping her heal, he told her how surprised he was by how fast she had healed herself. He said he'd never expected her to look so good so quick. Then he warned her, the roots of this break could come back to hurt her again someday.

Throughout this healing the girl felt her fear over how broken she had let herself become. She couldn't hide from the pain marking her and had to face herself every one of those days. Telling herself she could never become that broken again, she decided she'd never let herself be carried again. From that day on she said no to anyone who tried to carry her anywhere. During the few weeks it took for her face to heal, she could see everything, and she felt how she looked – broken.

## WHO BROKE THE GIRL?

Everyone she worked with could see how broken she looked, but she couldn't tell them how she had broken herself. She wanted them to see her as a strong woman who was good at her work, not the girl who needed to be carried. So she didn't tell them the truth about how she had fallen on the night she faced her pain. She told them she fell while out running. When told that, their shocked faces had questioned – "Who were you running from?" She laughed and never answered. The girl couldn't hear the truth in her own words, and she didn't know that she'd just started a run that wouldn't stop for years to come.

CRISTINA COSTANTINO

WHO BROKE THE GIRL?

☆
PART TWO
# WHERE THE GIRL RAN TO SEE
(YEARS: 27 - 33)

CRISTINA COSTANTINO

WHO BROKE THE GIRL?

☆
## HER LAST RUN IN THE WARM CITY

The girl ran her second friend out of their house and moved a new friend into her place. She couldn't let her second friend stay in her life, not after that night. She'd been left alone with her pain before and couldn't bring herself to try, once again, to fix what had been broken. Instead of holding on to what was already gone, she let go of their friendship. She couldn't see how her past was leading the choice she was making in this moment.

The new friend that moved in was curled tight in the right direction. They wouldn't live together long since the girl wouldn't live there much longer, not now that she'd started to run. But while there they enjoyed a run of good fun. Night after night they ran in to the same group, while they hopped from one bar to the next. Ending every one with a late night at one of their houses, they all piled up together for a sleepover, and then a morning run for a group breakfast.

With her second friend gone from her side, the girl pushed her close group of boys off to the side. She was starting to see that she wasn't, and didn't want to be, one of the boys. Her body told her when it gave out on her while she ran around with them, acting like she was one of them. It happened in the middle of her best play ever; during the tough game she loved to play with them. She jumped higher than she'd ever jumped before and stopped the other team's tallest boy, who was their toughest, right before he made a touchdown. Touching him, she stopped him. Then heard a snap when her feet landed. Her leg crumbled under her, no longer willing to support her in this sort of play. Taking her off the field, one of her boys picked her up to carry her for the last time, then went back to continue without her. She sat there and watched them, knowing she'd never play like one of them, with them or any others, again.

She couldn't move quickly for weeks after, but she kept herself moving. She moved her friendship away from the boys and closer to the group of girls she was already spending most of her nights with. She could see that these girls were different from her, but she saw how she had the most fun with them now, so she decided to play with them. She looked like she was having so much fun while she drank as much as they did with them, more than she really liked to drink. She looked like she was having so much fun while they visited a city painted in neon, a city too fake for her taste. She looked like she was having so much fun playing on their team in the game with the bases, the one she mostly sat through since her swings never connected. She knew she didn't like most of these girls all that much, but she really liked one of them, so much. She was the most fun out of all of them and the girl had the most fun with her.

The girl and this friend had so much fun together. They laughed themselves silly, straight to the ground, whenever they were together. They laughed while they ran together, ate together, drank together, and played together. The girl laughed with this friend more than she had ever laughed with anyone. Then one night the girl cried to this friend. She cried the night she ran in to the boy she had liked first after the broken boy, the night he told her he could never like her again. She'd already known but had hung on to the hope that things between them would someday be different. She only cried for one night. Then the girl and her friend went straight back to laughing.

She loved this friend as much as she'd loved her second friend, but this friend wouldn't be in her life long enough to become her third closest friend. Things changed too quickly for that to happen. Before the girl knew what had happened, this friend stopped calling, and the group stopped asking her to have fun with them. The girl guessed why this had happened even before she was told the reason. Her fun friend had started having fun with the boy she had liked first. The girl knew what would happen now, and she tried to stop it from happening. She told her friend she didn't care about any boy as much as she cared about her, and she didn't want to lose their friendship. If her friend was happy then she was happy for her. After that talk, she tried to keep having fun with her, but the friend, who she'd had the most fun with, couldn't have any fun with her now. There was too much guilt inside of her for her to have any fun with her.

So the girl moved her friendship over for the last time in the warm city. She went back to her group of boys, the ones that weren't hers anymore. Only, she didn't look like the happiest girl to them or with them anymore. She couldn't pretend she was one of the boys anymore. She could only be happy around them while with the other girls who were now friends with them. She spent time with these girls who were really good, and she had really good fun with them, but she couldn't have fun there much longer. She couldn't keep running around this city that was numbing her mind with its warmth that never changed and where she couldn't feel any happiness. She started wishing for a new life, and she wanted to run to a new city to find one. That's when she remembered one of her old wishes and decided it was time to go back there, back where they had first come from.

## WHO BROKE THE GIRL?

While she got herself ready to run to a new country, the girl, who wasn't feeling much of anything anymore, ran in to a new boy. A beautiful boy who had come from a country close to where she was going, one who didn't sound like any other boy she knew. This beautiful boy, who had just finished the studies he'd come to the warm city for, was about to move to a city half a world away. A city where no one would look like him or understand him. Once she made her move, this boy would be on the other side of the world from her, doing exactly what she was doing.

This beautiful boy gave her the dream she needed, one that could never be made real. A dream that was safe to have because it could never really hurt her. So the girl fell, after one week together, for this beautiful boy that she wouldn't be able to see for longer. She didn't know that she had only fallen for him because of the safety that came with him. She should have had a fun week and then moved on to someone new that lived in the new place she was moving. Not her, not now. She needed a dream to believe in that could never take her life over, one that would never make her fall over.

This beautiful boy would never try to make their dream real because his dream was to never grow up. He liked the feelings the girl gave him, and he liked sharing his with her, but that's all he wanted. So the boy, who didn't want to grow up, and the girl, who didn't want to risk her life, would share their lives with each other over the next year. Lives they wouldn't have to give up since there was a whole world to keep them apart, stuck safely in-between them. During this year they would share thousands of words that said nothing. Sweet words longing for something that neither of them knew wasn't really wanted. Sweet words that kept them both from feeling alone in their new worlds that were so different from them.

## A SMALL LIFE BACK THERE

Once the girl decided to go back where her parents had first come from, where they hadn't learned any good lessons, she learned a new lesson. It was a good one. She learned the hardest thing to do was to make a hard decision. Once the decision was made, everything she had to do to make it happen wasn't so hard. So she made her wish a reality, and she went back to live where they'd come from before they'd come over to live in the country she'd been born in. To meet the family she'd never met but had heard about throughout all the nights of yelling. To learn the language her parents had spoken to her, the one she understood but had never spoken back to them. To see the life they'd lived back there that was as different from hers as it was the same.

It took three months to make it happen. She worked to save, and she found work on the side so she could save more. She gave away everything she didn't want to carry there, and she stored everything she wasn't ready to let go of yet. She resigned from the work that made her happy, helping make beautiful work that she loved to see get made. The officials from back there, who lived over here, wrote her name down on some papers to say that she had come from them and belonged with them, so could live and work back there. She still didn't know where she would live, where she would work, who her friends would be, or if anyone would understand her. None of that mattered to her. She just knew she had to go back there.

So she left everything and everyone to start a new life back there. When she got there she found a girl to live with who'd been born and raised there, a stranger who didn't actually look like she was from there. This tall girl, with blonde hair and blue eyes, lived next door to the first friend she'd made when she was first born. Her friend looked like everyone from back there was supposed to look, like someday she was going to be someone's sweet little old mother. They may not have looked alike, but they both had the biggest smiles, and they filled her life with their brightness. As soon as they met her they made her one of their friends and changed her name to fit them. She still only went by the first half, but they made it smaller by cutting off a character, to make her sound like she'd come from there.

From the first day they opened their door, they opened up their lives to her and spent a lot of their time with her. At night they all cooked the food that was from there, then sat down together to eat it while talking across the table for hours. The girl, who hadn't known if she could speak their words, was rolling them off from the first day she got there. The group of girls acted silly together, like everyone there did, and made each other laugh while they sat around together. The girl, who had never wanted to look stupid, stopped caring how she looked and started to pick up their way of acting. A few times, they travelled to different spots in their country together, to relax in the bright sun by the sea. One time, they went down to show her their past, in they town where the two had been born next to each other. The girl was surrounded by more beauty than she'd ever seen before, and she couldn't believe how much clearer everything looked in this new life. The girl, who was full of a new bright feeling, loved the start of this life.

Then she went down farther on her own, to see where her family had come from. It was as far down as someone could go without dropping straight off into the deep end of the ocean. She went down to the bottom, and then over to the point poised to give a swift kick. That's where she met the last of the older ones for the first time. The one who hadn't taught her father the right lessons. This one looked at her the whole time, but she didn't have much to say to her.

The girl imagined she couldn't let go of the hurt she'd felt that her father hadn't brought her back sooner. But she didn't ask her, and she didn't try to talk to her, instead she chose to forget this one right after she met her.

Then she met the younger one, who was as old as her but smaller. The one she might have grown to be like if her parents hadn't moved their life away from there. When she first saw this one's life she liked what she saw. It was a life that looked happy, and it looked like the life she'd once dreamed would be hers if they hadn't moved from there. Then she took a closer look. The one she could have been didn't want to go as deep as the girl tried to pull her. This one liked the way she looked, and she couldn't see beyond what everything in this life looked like. One night she told the girl to change out of something that made her look different from them, and that made the girl see everything more clearly. No one there wanted to see anything outside of this life. They were happy enough, walking next to everyone they'd known across this life. Happy walking laps up and down the short road that ran between a rock wall on one side and short buildings, made out of rock, on the other. Passing the same rocks, and the same faces, night after night.

They were happy when nothing changed. The girl, who wanted to change, could never have been happy in that life. She was starting to see below the surface of this place her family had come from, and she didn't like what she was seeing. This place where people came to relax, was full of rules that kept everyone that lived there in line. Everyone tried to control everything that people did there. The girl saw where all the control that had once been put on her life had come from. She could now understand her family and the way they'd raised her.

The girl, who could understood how much more controlled her life would have been if they'd stayed there, called her mother to say – "Thank you for leaving." The mother, who had never made her speak like them while she was young and didn't like it when she spoke that way now, understood. Using the words from the country where she'd been born, the girl told her she was glad they'd given up their lives back there, back then, so she could have the one she'd had. The life she now understood had been the better one for her.

What she couldn't understand was why the friend she lived with, the friend she lived next to, and all their friends whom she'd met didn't choose to leave this life. She had been there long enough to hear enough, and the brightness of what had been shiny when new had faded. None of them sounded happy with the lives they had there. She could understand why, since they had to do a lot for their families and their way of working was broken. Almost no one worked at what they'd been taught, and those that did had to work for next to nothing. The girl grew tired of hearing about the systems that were broken beyond repair, so she told them to move to a place where they would have more control over their lives. They looked at her and smiled, they could never move. They wouldn't change where they lived because they couldn't change who they were. The girl couldn't understand them.

The girl who wanted to change wasn't like anyone there. Everyone thought she was, when they first saw her, because she looked just like them. Then they heard the truth as soon as she spoke their words. They could understand her, but she didn't sound anything like them. She used the same words as them to speak her thoughts, but she didn't know enough words to make all her thoughts understood by them. When she spoke the words she knew, she couldn't make enough of the right sounds to sound like them. She sounded broken when she spoke their words.

Her broken words worked well enough for her to work while she lived there. Within a month of her arrival she'd found work that sounded like it would be just like the one she'd had before. She made more then anyone there since she spoke her own language like an expert. She was happy at first, until she quickly realized the work she was doing wouldn't actually lead to anything. All they did was talk about making things. The girl couldn't work like that. She couldn't stand to do less than she had been; she needed to know she was working towards making something beautiful. That mattered to her too much to stay there. So she decided to leave the work that wasn't giving her what she needed to live. By now she didn't believe she could find what she needed back there that would work for her, and she didn't believe in the dream of a life there any longer.

## WHO BROKE THE GIRL?

She was done with this wish and ready to run from what wasn't working.

She decided, once again, that she wouldn't live a broken life any longer. She had gone back planning to stay for life, but she had gone back too far, too late, to make it her life. She had found work, but it took her too far away from what she was doing to make her happy. She had found friends, but she couldn't make herself understood enough to make her happy. She had found her extended family, but they seemed too small to make her happy. She made the decision to stop living back there after less than a year of that life. She decided to move again, so she could find a life that could make her happy.

That's when the girl made two decisions that would change her life twice over the next two years. She decided she wasn't done living a different life in a different place, but she didn't have the energy to be different again, just yet. So first she would go back to the city she knew. The city where she knew who her friends would be as soon as she got there. The city that had the energy she loved. With that decision made, she decided on her second move after that one, to another city in a country that was foreign. It was one where she didn't know anyone, but where everyone spoke the same language as her so she decided she could do it. She needed that second decision to be made so the first one wouldn't make her feel like she was giving up her dream.

After closing out this life and before moving on to her new one, she led herself to another ending. On her way over to the city with the best energy, she went out of her way to make a stop on the other side of the world. She went to see the beautiful boy who she'd seen so many beautiful words from every day she'd been away. She thought she knew him, and she thought she'd have a beautiful time in a beautiful place with him. But as soon as she saw him, she could see she wouldn't find any beauty anywhere near him.

He lived in a cold city filled with grey buildings, and the boy had a cold. He spoke to her with cold words the whole time she was spaced so close to him. The boy, who had been born in a country where everyone spoke a language filled with hard sounds, didn't even know he was being cold. He was being himself; the boy she didn't really know. The sweet words, safe to share from a distance, had disappeared into a cold distance between them. Now that they weren't a world away, he used his words to keep distance between them. She didn't find the beautiful time she'd been expecting, and she felt herself wake up from this dream she'd been having.

☆
## BACK TO HER LIFE

When the girl got back to the city that had the energy she needed, she lived with a girl who was family, even though she'd only met her once before and didn't really know her. She moved in with her big sister's new sister by marriage. They only had her sister in common, but like sisters who have nothing in common do, they found a common bond to connect them. They learned about each other while living together every day and driving back every few months to see the family they now shared. When they went back they spent time together with the one sweet little boy who was the nephew they shared between them. He'd started to talk and sweetly called her by the second half of her name, the half that sounded like a girl no one else knew. The girl needed this little boy's sweetness, and she needed this new sister, since she still hadn't let hers back into her life. Her new sister-friend acted like she didn't need anyone, but in this city where the girl had plenty, she didn't need anyone too much, so what they shared was enough for her.

As soon as she moved back to the city with all the energy, she went back to being known as half a boy, but she was a stronger girl now than she had been when she went by that name before. Even though she didn't like tough games anymore, or hanging out with the boys who played them. She only wanted to go out with boys who weren't from there and be friends with other girls who were. At a small reunion one of her old friends, who had once been a sister, didn't recognize her and said how different she was now that she was – "a firecracker." The friend, who had always been able to see her, was there and responded – "She was always like that."

Her old friends were in her new life, but they weren't her only close friends. Her sister-friend brought a friend from her past into her life. A girl, who didn't give herself enough to live, fully gave her friendship to the girl. These two girls became close fast. They broke apart, even faster, twice in this life, then once more later in life. But while they were close, this first time, they had fun together. They went out together every weekend, dressed like dolls and made taller by heels. Both girls liked to date the same kind of boys, the ones that hadn't been born there. They stayed

## WHO BROKE THE GIRL?

close while they ran from one place to the next, non-stop, in the same night.

Now that she was back in her city the girl lived close enough to her to become closer to the friend who had always been able to see her. This friend had a good life in the city she'd never left and was still close to the friend they had once shared. The one the girl had hurt by not attending her special day. They were connected through the one friend, so the girl decided to re-connect with the one she'd lost. She sent words of sorrow to the good friend she'd hurt while living with the broken boy. The friend heard the good in her words and accepted their friendship back into her life. The words put the past behind them, but their lives were too different now to be connected more than once in a while.

At first the girl stayed connected to the beautiful boy who wanted to send his beautiful words back over, now that she was a safe distance away. The girl, who had gone around the world to see him, started to see that there would only ever be words between them. She broke off their connection but it would take her a bit longer to break off the dream that he would make himself a real part of her life. This break broke something inside of her, the part that wanted to believe she could make anything she dreamed up happen. For the next year she would run from what had broken and jump from boy to boy. More boys in one year than she had been with in her life so far.

She was moving herself further away from who she was with what she was doing. It started with the one who she should never have known and should never have been with. She met him through the friend she went out with, the one who'd given her friendship to the girl. The two had dated, and then become friends. The girl broke what she believed in when she found herself with him in a way she'd never been with anyone so soon before, especially not someone a friend had once cared for. She didn't feel like she was making her own choice when she chose to act like someone she wouldn't have liked if she'd met. She couldn't see herself in what she'd done that made her feel so bad. What she'd done to her friend, that she believed was so bad. The girl, who stood for everything good, had done something she didn't believe in, and with that she didn't know who she was anymore.

This friend told her she didn't care; she only cared about their friendship. The girl could see what she'd done was the same that had been done to her by the friend she used to have the most fun with. So she knew that what her friend said about saving their friendship was true, but she was too full of guilt to see past it. She tried to break off their connection so she wouldn't see her own shame every time she saw her. They broke apart for a time, but this friend wouldn't let go of the girl who mattered to her. The girl never let go of her guilt, but she stopped looking at it so closely, and they became close friends again soon enough.

## WHO BROKE THE GIRL?

It only took a short time, but she wouldn't forgive herself for a long time.

This is about the time when the girl started to spend a lot of time at work. She gave herself over to it like she had once given herself over to the broken boy. She had so much work to do that she ran to get from one project to the next, as fast as her will could get her there. She ran from morning to night, and late into the night, to get it all done. This work was full of high energy, and she started to get a high from spending all of her energy there. Her work making stories that sold happy dreams took over all of her dreams. It became the only dream she felt safe having. This dream that she could control by how hard she worked, became all that mattered to her. She felt how much she mattered when she worked hard at something that she thought mattered so much.

The work that she loved doing was bigger than it had been in the warm city, and the people who did it were bigger. The time they had to do the work was shorter. The pressure to do more work was higher. The girl worked faster across more hours, but no matter how much she did it was never enough. Then she realized that whatever she did would never matter, not as much as before, and not as much as the ones who created the work. No one understood what people in her role did, or how much the space she created helped get the work made. The ones creating the work were the only ones who mattered. They made themselves matter, and everyone treated them like they mattered more than anyone. Not mattering first didn't stop her from doing this work. She had never let that matter before.

The girl made friends at work, but only made one into a close friend. A friend that she got together with after work and on the days they didn't have to work. This friend was just like her last work friend, the one who was still a friend. She was another one who was grounded and could help her stay grounded. Her time spent with this friend was always a solid good time. This friendship would never stumble across any rocks on the road, and they would never throw any rocks at each other.

The girl ran high on this life. High on the energy from the city she shared with all her friends, and high from her work. Then these highs started to drop her. The work that had driven her was making her crash, and she couldn't keep running as fast as she had been. Her mind would go numb, and her body would lean over, trying to force her to stop this run by taking her down. She kept standing by leaning on the grounded friend who kept her from hitting the ground, but her body wouldn't stop.

The girl, who had only gone to a doctor those other two times she'd fallen, went to one. He battered her with tests that didn't find anything that would cause her to fall over, but there was one thing he found that she'd never had before. There was a small hole in her heart. He told her that that wasn't what was hurting her head, but neither knew how wrong he was, and how much the pain in her heart was

## WHO BROKE THE GIRL?

hurting her life. He finally gave up on her and said that her work was making her panic. He told her to give herself time alone, sitting still, while keeping her mind quiet. She couldn't hear him. She didn't have time to sit still, not while there was so much work to run to.

She wouldn't stop what she was doing, but something stopped her long enough to read the beginning of a book that told her what she could do, now, to keep her balance by finding her own power. She liked how the man in the book had found his while he sat on a bench, paying attention to everything going on in the moment around him. She did what he told her over a couple of days that she wasn't at work, and she could feel the power coming through from inside of her. Then she went back to work and knew she had to choose between the two. She couldn't pay attention, like he had, and keep running as hard as she was. She chose her work over herself and packed the book away, but she didn't throw it away. She knew she would want to go back to it one day, when she could stop long enough to turn back to herself. For now, she kept running through this life every day, until she decided it was time to throw it away.

She was led to that decision after she was spurred to buy a piece of her own, new comfort. One she could sink down into, in full comfort. It was an expensive piece that would be hers to keep once taken home. Two burly men helped roll it a few blocks from the store to her door, only to realize, this comfort couldn't be squeezed into her life. The door it had to go through was too small, the angles too sharp to let so much comfort through. The men tried to help her, but their strength couldn't push it through. Asking them to wait, she ran to buy something sharp enough to saw away at its support, making it small enough to fit her space. When she got back she tried to hand it to them, but they told her she would have to do the work to break apart her own comfort. The girl tried, but it was too hard, so the two men took pity on her and did what they could for her, what she couldn't do, in that moment, for herself.

When her new, broken comfort was finally in she sank down into it, and under the weight of what felt like too much commitment to this life for her. It was a good life supported by good friends, but it was one she couldn't see herself in. She decided, within moments, that it was time to move on to the second life decision she'd made, before she'd come to live this one. She had to clear her vision to see more, so she decided it was time to leave this city, with all its comfort, behind. She wasn't ready to let go of her dream to live a different kind of life, not yet.

# A SECOND EXIT FROM HER CITY

With those papers she'd already gotten, that ones that said she belonged back where she'd lived and left, she could live in a lot of different countries. So she decided to move to the city she'd already picked because of the language they spoke, one big enough that she could keep working as hard as she already was. A city where she thought everyone would understand her as much as she needed to be understood. A city located across an ocean, one that would be new for her even though it was older than the city she was leaving.

Just like before, when she had moved herself back to where her parents had come from, her move across to this new-old city happened quickly. All it took was making the decision to move. Within three months of breaking off her comfort, she broke apart her life. This time she knew her work mattered too much to her to go without any. So she went over for one week, twice, to find a job where she could do even bigger work for even longer hours. Her second time over, she found an apartment to live in with two boys. These two had both moved there years earlier from where they were born in a country at the bottom of the world.

The family she kept moving away from wasn't happy with this move. The girl, who was afraid of hurting them, couldn't tell them how big a move this was that she was making. Knowing she was going with the dream to live there for a long time, maybe for the rest of her life, she decided a softer truth would be easier for them to handle. So she told them her work was sending her to live there for the next few months. She could hear in their voices that they had heard the hard truth behind her words. They knew she was going to be on this run for a lot longer than she was telling.

The girl didn't understand why, but she knew she had to leave this life she'd been living behind. To live in a world she didn't know, with people who didn't know her. To know something different from the life she knew so well. To see everything more clearly than she could while sunk in so much that was so familiar. To live somewhere that she could be different. She would get to know herself better because

## WHO BROKE THE GIRL?

of this next life, but before she could do that she would lose herself to the work that mattered to her more than she did. She would work harder than ever there, all the while telling herself it was ok to kill herself for work that wasn't doing anything for her.

Before she left to go kill herself, and while she was killing her life in her city, she killed the connection to her friend, the one who hadn't wanted to let go of her. It happened the last night she was in her city, when everyone got together to celebrate her: the old friends that used to be her sisters, her sister-friend, her friend who hadn't let go, her two grounded friends, and a few others from the fringes. The girl, who didn't know how to be celebrated, could see that the one friend wasn't celebrating as much as the others. This friend left her, before she was ready to go, to get to the next place they were going to celebrate.

She chose to leave the girl, who was leaving her behind, before she left. The girl felt like she didn't matter to her now that she was leaving. Getting to the next place they were going that night, where the friend would have more fun, mattered more to her than the girl. The girl, who didn't know she mattered, yelled at her friend when she got there. The friend yelled back, telling her – "It's not all about you." The girl, who already knew that, still knew that yelling wouldn't change anything, but she let out the yells driven by the fear of the change she was making.

The next day, the girl who had gotten rid of everything walked all the roads she was making herself give up. While walking, fear of the new road she was facing came up from inside and tried to freeze her in her tracks. She couldn't remember why she'd decided to leave this life for one she didn't know. To leave her city for one she didn't know. To leave her close friends to go where no one would be close to her. She stomped her fear down by telling herself she'd made her choice, and she had to live with it. The girl, who knew how to keep to a choice once made, made her move.

WHO BROKE THE GIRL?

☆
## ACROSS TO A NEW-OLD CITY

The girl was a stranger in this new-old city where she went to live with strangers. She landed on her own that first day, carrying six large cases that overwhelmed her as she rang the door of the new home called a flat. One of the two men she was going to live with, the one she hadn't met yet, came down to let her in, and she was taken aback by his tall, golden appearance. She accepted the strength he offered and let him carry everything for her without thinking twice. She saw how good this one was right away and the more she saw the more she liked how good he was to her the whole year they spent as flatmates. She barely saw the one that was never there, so the two shared the whole space and it became a home that two friends lived in.

Despite how comfortable he made her, she felt strange in this new life. Her mind, used to moving fast, had gone completely empty. The girl, who was used to change, was in shock from how her life had changed so much, so fast. Even though she had changed so much, so fast, a few times already. All the new people around her sounded strange to her. Their words were the same as hers, but she still couldn't understand them. She couldn't understand what anyone wanted her to do when directed with the words that sounded the same as hers but had a different meaning. When she was told to - "bin it" - she could only stare blankly. Even if she had understood what they meant, it wasn't easy for her to throw anything away. The girl, who was far away from anyone who cared about her, misunderstood everything. When asked, with voices that sounded caring – "How are you?" any time she said – "Hi" to anyone, she was surprised that they cared enough to ask. Before long she realized they asked everyone that same question, the one asked with no desire for a real response.

She didn't recognize anything around her in this new-old city. Everything looked close to the same as where she'd come from, but she could see the differences. She felt more alone than she'd ever felt anywhere she'd ever lived. The roads looked empty in this place that had been a lot of small towns before it was turned into one big city. She couldn't feel any energy bouncing off of anything around her. Every day she walked down those roads on her way to work, her mind would shift back to see the old roads she'd left behind. It made her sick, how much she missed the roads she used to walk down, but she hid that sadness and gave a cheer back to everyone she came across.

Everyone in this new world liked her. They told her. Even though they didn't like most of those from her part of the world. She knew how to laugh. They told her. Even though no one from her part of the world was funny. She spoke with a good, quiet tone. They told her. Even though everyone from her part of the world spoke too loudly. The girl, who didn't like to stand out, only showed them the parts of her that were most like them. She started to speak so softly that she nearly whispered herself away. She started to make them laugh; in the same way they made her laugh, the way that was meant to cut one with its cleverness. She started to change and they changed her name to make it flow quicker. She wasn't known as half a boy any longer. She became known by the sound of the broken circles that made up her two initials.

The girl, who didn't know how to give up easily, wouldn't give up on this new life where she didn't feel much comfort. She worked hard to make it work. Even before she started to understand anyone in this city, she understood what one of the ones paying for their work wanted. This one lived in a different place, the same one the beautiful boy had first come from. Like him she had a cold distance to her and spoke with hard sounds that were tough to understand.

## CRISTINA COSTANTINO

On a call in one of her first weeks there, the girl told her that something she wanted done was impossible. In her hard voice, she commanded – "That is your challenge. Get me what I want."

The girl, who believed she could do the impossible, now that she had made two impossible moves, worked harder than she had ever worked before to make this life work. She was determined to stay in this dream but needed to go back to the comfort of her old life as much as possible that first year so she could keep going. When she went back she would split her time between her family in one city and her friends in another. She would see the family who missed her and felt happy in her short time with them. Then she would go to see all her friends and would feel even happier, until she had to leave them. Their city still felt like hers, and she could feel all of its energy holding on to her. Every time she pulled herself away the sadness poured out of her. She pushed the sadness down every time and made the same choice, sticking to the choice to leave it behind.

Before too long she made a friend at work, a woman who was different from her last two work friends. This one was like the friend who used to lead her; she led everyone around her everywhere. This woman was younger than the girl but acted older, and since she still felt like a girl this woman could easily lead her. She had a lot of friends there, even though she had just moved there herself, so she was just what the girl needed.

## WHO BROKE THE GIRL?

This lead friend played harder than anyone the girl had ever been friends with before, and she led them out from hours in bars to hours in clubs to even later afterhours. Never knowing where their nights would end, some nights not knowing where they were when they ended them. She led the girl to a new high that the girl had kept herself from being led to before. The girl wouldn't let herself be led there too much, but plenty enough. In the short time she lived there this friend would always lead everyone in her big group of friends to gather together. She led herself back to her last city soon enough, but before she left she led the girl to her new third closest friend. One that she would love even more than she had loved the first two.

This third friend, who ate up every moment of the life she loved, took over where the friend from the warm city, who the girl had once had the most fun with, had left her. They started having the most fun together the last day of the year, half a year after the girl had moved to this new-old city. She loved all the time she spent with her third friend in this life that had started to feel like hers. Time spent sitting up high in random red buses they picked to get on, that took them anywhere it chose to go, while they imagined up a story about anyone walking down below. Time spent walking all the cobbled roads around the one common green spot set in-between their two homes. Time spent drinking cold wine while sitting in the hot sun, talking to anyone friendly sat nearby. Time spent staying up all night while dancing in every spot they landed. Time spent drinking tea all the next day, while talking about their night.

They grew tight, but the girl wasn't going to be one of two like she had been before. She was going to be one of two, times two. At the same time, she made friends with a girl who used to work where she now worked. This one was like her in ways her third friend wasn't, and the girl loved her so she made this one her fourth closest friend. Like with her third friend, the girl had a lot of fun with this fourth friend who was so funny. Just like the girl, this one had pieces inside of her that had been broken back in her past and they'd both made their lives work around these breaks. The girl loved being around this friend who got so high off her own energy. At times she loved her as much as her third friend who loved life, and at times more, but then there were times it was less.

The girl didn't feel any less for her until after they moved to live in one new place together. She left the tall boy she'd been living with behind to be with a tall girl he met through her, one she'd met at work and he would eventually make his wife. She had introduced the two of them knowing they would love each other's light. The girl loved living with someone who was good to her, but he needed his space to be one of two, and she needed to live with a girl.

The girl and her fourth friend had to climb plenty of short steps up two steep flights to get to the flat they shared that let the brightest light shine down on them. This flat was near a high road that she loved to walk down. At times, they laughed a lot and shined together under that brightness. Only, a lot of rain poured down from the clouds in this new-old city that they lived in together. Like the sun, their laughter would come to a stop more often than the girl liked, but eventually it would always come back. It only came to a full stop later, when the broken pieces inside of the two came up to break them apart and make their friendship go flat.

Even when it was light her third and fourth friends never shined next to one another. She tried to bring them together, to make them one whole unit, but she had to give up and learn how to bounce between them. They were the two parts of her life that were so similar, yet too different. She could never understand how she could like them both so much when they didn't like each other at all. She spent most of her time having fun, whether out or in, with her third friend. She mostly had fun with her fourth friend when they were both inside the flat they had in common. She would have gone out with her and her friends, but that would have brought her closer than her fourth friend wanted.

She didn't understand why they had started out strong and then weakened. Only seeing each other when they both happened to be home at the same time. She'd lived with strangers who'd become friends plenty, but never with a friend who kept this kind of distance between them. That was strange to her. She had moved in with her to share time, not just space, with a friend. The girl was hurt, but she made herself understand. She needed her fourth friend in this city where she didn't have many. Her fourth friend, with all her energy, had plenty here and didn't need her all that much. What she needed was her space. Things would break down between them when her friend's energy got low, then she needed space around her to charge back up. This made the girl cautious; scared to tread heavy, in case she cracked the shell her friend had placed around her. Despite their difficulties, they kept their friendship alive, even though it was hard for the girl to keep her balance in this friendship.

In all, she'd grown to love this new life she was building. She loved laughing with her friends and laughing while at work. Harder then she was used to laughing. She loved drinking with her friends and drinking with her team at work. More than she was used to drinking. She loved being more connected to this city through her friends, and more connected to the world through work. More than she had ever been before. The girl had found her comfort in this new world.

She even started to sound like she belonged where she was living. Her voice said the words she hadn't understood when she first got there, and it had a different sound to it. Her words came out softer, and every thought was sung into a question. When she went back to her old city everyone questioned her. They asked how she could sound like she was from across there when she had just started living there. She didn't sound exactly like that. She sounded like she was from somewhere in-between both of her worlds. She kept living in her in-between world, and she loved it, until she didn't have enough time to love anything any longer.

CRISTINA COSTANTINO

☆
# THE WORLD THAT NEVER STOPPED

The girl never stopped in this new world. The energy she'd lost at first was back and it carried her everywhere. She found the energy inside of her and started giving it all out to this new life she was living. To the few good friends she'd made and the few boys she made out with when she went out all night with her friends. Most of all she gave her energy to all the hard work she was doing, without knowing she was giving away all her good energy.

Her work, that had already been hard, had gotten harder. So she worked harder. Then some work she did throughout the day and night across one weekend made the ones that worked up high look over at her. They saw how she made herself work so they chose her to do the biggest work they needed done. Her work, the one that made her feel like she mattered, made her matter even more. Overnight, she started working with everyone who lived across the world. One of the ones high up told everyone that she was the girl who never let any of many balls drop. Hearing that, she worked even harder, across every day and night of this life, to keep any balls from slipping. Now that every one of her nights was someone else's day somewhere, her work never stopped.

She started running harder, and she never stopped running. No one told her to stop. This work wouldn't, it only told everyone to – "Be better." It didn't matter how good your work already was or what it took out of you to make it better. The ones up high had thrown her the work and now it was up to her to make it work, without sinking. They only looked back over when they had more work to hand her. They gave her a few people to do the work with, but it wasn't enough, even though they were ones that worked hard and that she liked working with. A group of girls worked hard under her to create the space that helped the work get made. A group of boys worked hard next to her while they created the work that was more beautiful, and mattered more, than anything she had helped get made before.

Then a man, who knew how to lead creative to be smarter, put himself on her work because he knew how much it mattered and that it was a smart move for him to be on it. He knew they weren't just creating one small story that sold a dream. They were creating the deeper meaning behind every story that was being sold across the world. This work mattered so much that the girl decided to make this work be what mattered the most for the next year of her life. She didn't know it would go on for two years and that she'd made the choice to give all of herself over to this work.

The man, who would become her closest partner in creating this work, knew how to destroy. No one wanted to work with this man who wouldn't bend to their will, and at first the girl hated working with him because of how much he forced everyone to bend. Raising her voice, the girl spoke to this man louder than she had to anyone she had ever worked with. From the small room papered with the story they were creating out to the big room lined with rows of ears to hear them. The two argued constantly. Everyone could see these two did good work together and could hear they were headed straight to the day when one would kill the other.

Despite all this hard work, the girl still found some time to have fun at work with the small group around her and out of work with her third and fourth friends. She went out with a few boys, a few times each, but she was working too hard to make any one of them matter. She felt relieved not to have one boy she wanted to be with more than she wanted to do her work. She didn't want that pull, not when she needed to work. After the day that celebrated her 32$^{nd}$ year, the day that made her feel her age for the only time ever, she put more focus on work and made a ridiculous declaration – "By this point I'm waiting for my husband to get divorced anyways so I minus well work."

She was running so hard without looking up that she lost herself in all of her work. Her body knew what she was doing, and knowing better than her, wanted her to stop pushing so hard. Just like before it tried to stop her. Her arms went numb to try to stop her from punching the keys of her computer so quick. Her mind went foggy to try to stop her from thinking so much. Her eyes poured out water to try to stop her from seeing how much work she still had to weed through. She wouldn't stop for long, but was routinely forced to stop for a moment, before she forced herself to go straight back to work. Those moments of pausing wouldn't stop coming.

During the few moments she wasn't running, her mind tried to break through the fog to warn her. While walking to work, it would repeat the same headline to her – "The girl was killed." When pausing for a moment, while running at work, the words would pop up in her mind – "There's nothing left of me. All I am is this work." No one could hear her, but everyone could see she was running herself to death. The ones up high didn't look too closely at what she was doing since she was doing exactly what they needed her to do. They waited until she was done with enough of their work before showing her any worry. They told her to

## WHO BROKE THE GIRL?

stop working and go home the late night that ran out after the long day before it, that had been run straight into from the night before, that had run straight out of the early day that had started her longest work day ever.

Work sounded like it cared that night, and then again months later when it let her leave it behind for three weeks of no work. Those were the weeks she had to live her life. When she got back, all rested, work greeted her with more work. Making her feel like she mattered even more than she already had, but not more than she really did, just more than she still knew. She was being rewarded with the work that she had always wanted, that she couldn't bring herself to say no to taking. Work making something beautiful that would be seen from screen to screen.

Only, she still had a lot of work to do getting the rules in place to protect the deeper story that they had already sent out to all of their offices to work with. Everyone was starting to create off of this story, and they weren't getting it right. The one paying all of them was angry, so the ones high up in the main office she worked in told their world that the head creative and the girl had to see all their work before anyone paying them saw anything. The girl read the note that had gone out and said goodbye to her life.

She started to give out the energy she had just filled up to all of this work. Her one foggy mind started working between three streams of work. Every day and night, for nine months, she ran through all of this work; creating one beautiful story, writing the rules over all the stories and urgently seeing everyone's stories, around the clock, from around the world. Everyone was working too hard in the small group she worked with. They were all doing double duty, running through their days and into their nights together, trying to get all the work done.

The man she had once fought became her closest friend at work. They'd stopped fighting each other and started fighting off everyone together, to protect the work they both believed in more than anything. Her and the boys, who were creative, pushed each other forward, laughing while they pushed. They gave her a lot of support, and she always turned to them for more. She could forgive them anything, even when they did something that made her have to work harder. The girls in the group she led were so good, and tried so hard to offer her their support, but it was never enough for the girl who worked too hard. She couldn't forgive them that she chose to do more work than them. She did it to get it done faster and keep them from feeling overworked. She couldn't hear how she had started to silently blame them for how much she overworked herself. She barely whispered it, but they heard her bitterness loud and clear.

☆
## **DONE WITH KILLING**

The last of the energy inside her went out when they tried to give her more work when she already had too much to do and more support wasn't being given. That's when she told them. While sitting with the boy who wanted everything she was in charge of, the man in charge of her, and the man who would soon be in charge of everyone, she said – "I'm done." She stood herself up on those two words. She was ready to walk away from them and the work that was killing her, but she still wasn't done killing herself.

When the top creative, in charge of all the creative teams across the world, heard the news, he told everyone sat on the board beside him – "We can't lose her." It was too late. They had already lost her. Even though she was done with them, she couldn't go anywhere anytime soon. When she had first started working for them they'd made her promise to stay, even once she wanted to leave, for much longer than she would have ever chosen to on her own. For three months after the girl was done, she had to keep working. She'd promised to wait until they found someone to take over all of her work, but they never even looked for someone who could never do what she did. During this time the girl, who used to give them all of her time, started taking her time back. Looking up from her work, she looked around to see what everyone else was doing, and decided it was what she would do too.

She decided to go. She would take her life back by taking some time off work. Instead of helping make work that was beautiful, she wanted to go somewhere beautiful, somewhere she had never been before. Somewhere that had no work that needed to be done. She wanted to spend all her time seeing the beauty she had never had time to see before. Only, she didn't want to see it alone. The girl, who had moved alone twice, never wanted to go somewhere alone again. So she was happy when her fourth friend, who had been tired out by her work, decided to go with her. They agreed to take their energy somewhere new together. She wanted to make the move as soon as her last day of work was over, but her friend needed more time to make things work. The girl didn't know that the time it took to make this move would nearly kill her.

Even though she had let go of her hard work, the girl still wasn't at ease. She would have to wait until she got herself further from this time, and farther from this place, for her energy to come back to her. While she waited for that, something happened. The man, who she'd hated before he became a close friend, had become something she needed. A friend who saw how much light their work took from her and hated them for it. He could feel for her since his own light was dying because of what had become hard in his life. While they worked together she thought they were helping keep each other's light shining. She couldn't see when he started helping himself to the rest of hers to try to save his.

The girl, who'd completely broken down, couldn't save herself from this. Her work, that she had run herself into the ground with, had run her too close to him. One of the last nights of her last week of that work, he told her – "I love you." She'd never thought of love when she was with him before, but now she thought, maybe she did love him. She was so lost by then that no one, not even the girl, could know what she was really feeling. She felt how tired she was of fighting and how much she needed to be loved, so she let him love her. The only thing she really knew, through the fog of her exhaustion, was how bad this felt and how much foggier it made her. She walked through this fog of pain every one of the last days that she walked through this life. He wasn't supposed to love her, he was supposed to love the one he'd committed his life to, and she didn't want to love someone who belonged with someone else. She knew she wasn't helping herself by being with him. She was killing off the last of the light inside her.

His mind used his grey logic to turn her heart upside down, so she would give him what he needed. No time together was clear of his conviction that she didn't need what she needed, which was to get away from him and live in the light. The girl, who always loved giving, didn't like giving love like this. Having to hide all the love she had and hide herself. Hidden in the name he gave her, the name he chose for her because it was the same as a food he savored. She tried to make him see her truth, but he couldn't see what this was doing to her. She needed him to let go of her before he ate up all of her light. She tried hard to let go, and failed harder, every day of every week, over those last three months she lived there. So she waited for the day to come when she would be able to get away from this place where she was dying.

She couldn't stop herself, and couldn't see herself in what she was doing. Something she knew wasn't good, and that she didn't believe in, once again. She couldn't stand having anyone see her, now that she could see that there was a side of her that could do this. Her fault was so clear to her, and all of her faults poured out of her. She felt the shame she knew the world would put on her, and her shame drove her to beat herself down further. He couldn't understand her since he could live in the grey, but she couldn't live anywhere except in the light. She knew she would lose the last of herself if she didn't get away, far away, from this shadow that was swallowing her. She struggled, while waiting for the time to come when she could go where she thought the light would shine down brightly on her.

CRISTINA COSTANTINO

☆
## **CUTTING CORDS**

Before she could leave, and while she was still tied to the dying, she started to do what she had to, and cut the cords that bound her to this life. She cut her ties to the third friend who she didn't want to say goodbye to. The two that had laughed, ate, talked, danced and ran together across this life. The girl didn't want to leave her behind so she had to put space, that hadn't been there before, between them. It happened while they were both visiting her city that had all the energy. The girl went there to say hello to her old friends before she said goodbye to everyone, and her second friend's sister had brought her there to celebrate her. The girl was happy to bring everyone together – her old friends, her second friend, and the sister. Everyone shined together, talking through their laughter while they ate and drank together.

The girl spent one of these days back in her city being a tourist with the two sisters. They wandered from the top to the bottom and over to each side. Laughing the whole time they wandered. Her third friend, who loved every minute, floated through the streets in a sundress the girl had lent her. While she wore it one of the straps that held it up tore off, but the girl didn't care. She loved sharing something of hers with someone she cared for. The sun shined down brighter and brighter until the girl, who had gotten used to the clouds in the new-old city, felt like she was melting.

In the middle of their bright day the friend found a shop that had beautiful dresses just like the one she was wearing. She tore through them in her happiness. Then she tore off the dress she had on, the one with the torn strap that had picked up dust during their wander and had started to fade under all the brightness. She crumbled it up without a glance and shoved it down into the new bag she was given. She didn't need it, not now that she had a new dress to put on. The girl didn't say a word, but she felt the pain it pricked inside of her. The dress she had loved sharing wasn't worth anything now. She had worn it until it was worn out, and then easily replaced it, even before their day came to its end.

The second friend didn't notice the tension in the space growing between them. She was too busy seeing everything new that was around her, captured in all the shots she was snapping. Blow-by-blow she captured every step her sister and the girl took in the city she loved as much as the girl did. The girl covered her face at times, but mostly didn't mind. She did ask, maybe too much, to look at the shots to see how they had turned out. At the end of the day she saw a few whose angle made her look a way she didn't want anyone to see her. She couldn't stand seeing herself in this poor light. She asked her friend to delete them so no one else would see her like that. That made her friend snap – "No! That's what you look like."

The girl was wounded by the shot, but didn't say anything. They said goodbye to each other without a word about how their day was ending. The friend and her sister left to go back to the city they lived in, and the girl stayed a few days longer. Then she went back to spend a little more time in the new-old city before she went to the new place that would have all the shine she needed. The two friends, who had been so close, wouldn't spend that last bit of time together. They met once for one single exchange. With no words of sorrow from either, the third friend gave the girl back the dress that had been lent to her. Cleaned up but still half torn, the girl would never wear that dress again. She couldn't stand to look at what had once been beautiful that was now faded.

They wasted the time that they could have been having fun together keeping themselves away from each other. Instead of sharing the last days with the friend she was leaving, she spent it running around the new-old city with her fourth friend, sharing the best energy they had ever had between them, preparing for where they were going to wander together. The fun they'd had before, in-between the broken moments, had grown into a good stretch of time, and they had grown closer. The girl couldn't wait for when they would go away together.

Before they went the girl would go back to her third friend, right before it was too late, to say a goodbye that was good for both of them. The girl knew she didn't want to leave their friendship behind forever, even though she was leaving her for now. They met, forgave each other quickly, and ran back into their friendship for the few days left to them. Then the girl packed up the last of her things and asked to leave a few boxes with her for safekeeping. She left the boxes with instructions for her third friend to wear anything she wanted, however much she wanted, while the girl was away from them.

Right before the end she called to cut the family who thought she'd already run as far as she could get. They had no idea how far she'd been planning on running. She told them a week before she left that she was leaving for the trip she'd been planning for six months. She told her mother one night and asked her to break it to her father for her. She told her how badly she needed to go without giving her a reason. Her mother was scared for her, but she knew she didn't have the strength to stop her.

## WHO BROKE THE GIRL?

Then the call came, in an early hour of the next morning. The father, who used to yell, cried out to her not to go. Scared, he told her – "You could die if you go there." She couldn't tell him she would die if she stayed. He gave up trying to convince her as quickly as he started. Even if he'd had more time, he couldn't have changed her mind. Begging her to save him from his fears for her wouldn't change what she had already decided to do.

The girl cut off everything she was leaving behind, and then she got a cut from the fourth friend who was leaving with her. The two friends, who had their own broken pieces inside, fell out right before they left together. In the time they had waited for this time away, her friend had fallen for a boy she didn't want to leave behind. As the day of departure approached she pushed the girl away, and the girl felt the blame in her push. The blame for a trip that the fourth friend said she still wanted to go on.

Instead of blaming the trip that was taking her way from her boy, she told the girl she didn't like living next to her choices. The choice to see a man the friend knew she shouldn't be seeing. The choice to stop working while her friend chose to keep working until the last day there. The girl felt the tension stuck in the air between them, and by the time they left for their trip the two were barely speaking.

They still stuck to their plan and cut the hold they had on their bright flat, stored everything they owned in one small room, and left everyone behind. They left to go wander in a place that was supposed to be shining bright by the time they got there, but it would be a place where the pounding rain would follow them to almost every one of their stops. The girl was afraid to go with her now that the brightness between them had faded, but she would live the choice she'd made, that's one of the things she was good at. They left to go somewhere far from any life she'd ever known. The girl thought they had prepared for anything that might come their way across the four months they would spend wandering as far south and east as they could get. She hadn't known that the only thing that would hit her while there was who she was bringing with her.

WHO BROKE THE GIRL?

☆
## TRAVELLING TO SHINE

The two girls who used to share a home were now two girls with five outfits each, stuffed into packs they carried on their backs. Sleeping wherever they found a room that sold itself by the night, they moved themselves every week so they could see something different. Never deciding where their next stop would be until they were ready to leave the one where they were. The girl felt light in this freedom. There was nowhere she had to be, nothing she had to do, and no one to please for months ahead of her.

Only, she hadn't left everything weighing her down behind. She'd left the grey man behind forever, that was for sure. Saying goodbye to that death, she would never re-live it, while away or after she went back. She wasn't weighed down by those feelings, but her friend, who used to have high energy, had been flattened by her feelings for the boy she had to leave behind. The girl who'd felt plenty of sadness understood her feelings. She felt her friend's sadness, and she tried to lift her higher. She didn't care about the falling out they'd had before leaving, and didn't want to carry that energy around with them, but no matter how much she tried to keep things up, they kept falling.

This sadness wasn't the only weight they carried to every stop. They carried the weight of their closeness. When they lived in their bright flat that had a lot of space, the girl had been able to give her friend the space she needed, and had learned when to give it to her. She had given a lot right before they left, but there was no longer any to give. They were together every day that they shared wandering, and every night that they slept in the same bed. The girl liked the closeness of this spacing that she didn't know she needed, but her friend couldn't get the space she needed, and the tension that came with that wore on both of them.

They started their travels weighed down in a country that her friend looked like she could have been from. The country with the city, where they first landed, that looked like bombs had landed on it. The girls started walking its streets in the early hours while millions still slept in its slums. That first day, everything scared her. Fear hit her when a man, seeing their packs, forced them off their walk along the side of the building he was protecting. Leaving them to walk in the middle of the road where the stray dogs were roaming. Fear hit her when another man passing by promised to make them famous if they came with him. A little bit of fear even hit her when the little boy came up to them with foam covering the mouth he was brushing with one hand while the other lifted, asking for their money. Finally, the most fear hit her after they'd agreed to let another man lead them to a guesthouse they could catch up on their sleep in. Yet another man answered their knock on his door and led them through his dark hallways, past a guest dead asleep on the floor, to a room that could be padlocked from them on the inside or him on the out. The girl worried herself to sleep after questioning her choice to come and thinking the only answer was to run back to the home she'd already given up. Then she woke and found her courage in the light, and was ready to walk straight into this new life.

She was going to walk a lot of steps while there, and she was going to write words about every one. The girl, who still didn't know the story about the girl on a road, started writing stories about this wander. At first, so she could feel like she was still working at something during these months that didn't hold any work for her. Then her words took her over, and she fell for how it made her feel while writing them. She started to let herself dream a big dream, but only a little. Wondering if her stories could start a new life for her, one spent wandering to write what she saw. Only, she couldn't see this dream clearly, even though it felt like a good one for her. She couldn't see herself writing for other people, who told her what to write by when. She was sure that would kill her words and any happiness around them. So she decided to only live this dream while she was free, when she could have it for herself.

She kicked her writing off with stories about their life in that first country, where the women wouldn't stop trying to sell to them and the men wouldn't stop looking at them. The country where her friend had trouble adjusting, not able to see herself as clearly when everyone saw her as one of them. The girl saw how hard her friend was working to show everyone who she was, someone that wasn't anything like them, even though she looked somewhat like them. She always wore loose shirts that were ripped enough to show the bright material of the support that held her. She wore shorts that were super short, so the legs that held her up could feel all the brightness when it shined down on them. The girl could see that this was working against them. The men looked at them harder, and groups of them started to wander behind them while looking at them. The looks bothered the girl who had never wanted that much attention on her, but she didn't blame her friend. She yelled at the men, and then started to dress like her.

They were looked at in all six places they stopped, as they crossed half that country in their first three weeks. They were looked at in trains they rode overnight. Stuffed with as many people sleeping inside as were hanging on outside and lying across its top. They were looked at in the trains they took during the day, while they watched trash being swept up by little arms that were attached to a little body that swept those arms up at the end and held them out for their money. They were looked at on broken old buses. Crammed with people standing too close to the two girls that had gotten to their seats before them. The girl, who was always being pushed, always moved herself over closer to her friend, only to find herself getting pushed even more. She always moved as close as she could, and her friend always told her to stop moving so they would stop pushing. They were looked at while they rode in small cars that were more like big bikes. With no straight lanes they swerved from side to side, throwing the girls against each other, always just missing the other big bikes, people and animals that were coming straight at them.

They never swerved into anything, and they almost never wandered into anyone like them. Except in the one spot that gave the girl more peace than any spot she'd ever been in before. That's where they met the two men who took them to the two places that gave off the most peaceful energy ever. The first was made out of one tree with deep roots that had grown up as far as they could see, turning it into its own forest of trees. In this one tree-forest the girl climbed weightless. She went up high and sat herself down, cradled in peace. Touching the tree, she felt its peace pump into her.

Standing back on the ground, they went over to jump the field of boulders that was equally endless. Jumping from boulder-to-boulder until all they could see surrounding them were more boulders to jump. The girl felt the weight of her shorter legs there, and she looked to the tall one who guided them to help her when she had to jump farther than she thought she could on her own. His kindness never refused her, and with his helping hand she made every jump. Then they guided the girls down underneath the boulders. Down there, cradled by boulders, the girl touched one and it handed her its peace.

The two friends made their peace in this country with all the peace. They hadn't looked at any of their troubles close enough to clear them out, and the girl could still feel the tension lying low in between them, but for now their energy was jumping. The girl knew that her friend was still too sad, couldn't see herself clearly, and was spaced too close to her for comfort, but there was so much else to see that she chose not to look at any of that. Even without looking, these things would keep popping up until the two reached the end of the time they would be close friends.

## WHEN THE GIRL LED HERSELF

The two girls next jump was to the country where the friend's family had originally come from, and where the girl would lose some of her peace before jumping out of. They arrived in its biggest city but only stayed long enough to understand that everyone wanted to scam them. They knew it when the man who picked them up, to drive them around, wouldn't let them out unless they gave him more than the price they'd agreed. They knew it when the friend's family, the one who still lived there, asked for more than the friend could give. They knew it when the boys, who had seemed nice when they first offered to take them around, tried to get more than the friendship the girls wanted to give.

Standing their ground with all of them, their last night out with the boys sent them out in a torrential downpour, to search for a ride back to the guesthouse they would check out of within a couple of days. Sick of being scammed, they jumped on a train that rattled their teeth for the three hours it took to get to the peace they needed by the country's water.

That's where they met the boy visiting from a country situated next to a different body of water. They met him one night while they played the card game they always played, the one with the rules the girl had never known and that her friend made up from memory. He played while talking to them both, and the girl, who was used to coming in second, was sure he liked talking to her fourth friend better. They played a few quick games before he left to come back with his friends later that night. That's when he showed them his decision. He had chosen to like the girl best. The girl liked the attention, and both girls liked playing with him and his friends that night, so they met them for breakfast the next day, followed by dinner the next night. The boy kept paying the girl more and more of his attention.

They all kept playing together while the two paid even more attention to each other and then started to play around together. That's when her fourth friend told her she was going to leave to meet the boy she missed who was coming down for one week to work one country over. She would meet back up in the next country that they'd already booked plans to get to. Only it would be later than planned.

## WHO BROKE THE GIRL?

The girl wanted her friend to do whatever would make her happy, and she was happy that she would get to see her boy, but she was afraid to go to a big city on her own. After sleeping on it overnight, she told her friend what she had decided to do that would make her happy. Instead of moving on, she would stay where she was, close to this new boy and his friends, for the time her friend was with her boy. Her friend didn't like that decision.

The girl never understood what made her friend so upset with her. She wanted to stay by the water and have fun in a group, more than she wanted to sit in a city that might scam her, while she waited for her to come back to her. No words were spoken at first, but the girl could feel the tension growing in the small space between them. She asked her friend to talk to her about what she was feeling, and that's when she heard what she couldn't understand. The friend said the girl was leaving her for a new boy she had just met. She didn't want to hear it when the girl replied – "But you're the one leaving me."

The girl couldn't make her understand, so she made herself travel seven hours to get to a spot the friend said she had wanted to go to before leaving this country. The girl went with her so she wouldn't have to go alone, and she stayed with her for one day and two nights. Then she spent seven hours getting back to the spot she had never wanted to leave in the first place. The friend stayed for another two days on her own. She told the girl later, in short pops, that she was upset she'd been left alone there.

CRISTINA COSTANTINO

The girl knew her friend wasn't happy with her, but she was happy with her choice. She wasn't alone in a city she didn't know. Instead, she was feeling happy, shining bright with the water in front of her and this boy next to her. This boy from another country belonged to a people that felt deeply and always told everyone exactly what they were feeling, as loud as they felt like. It was only one week that they were together, but from the first to the last they told each other how they felt, just like any close couple would. From morning to night, and then all through the night, the girl spent her time with this boy who let her touch his feelings. They spent plenty of time alone and plenty with his friends, and every minute was spent laughing.

Only, the girl, who had felt this before, started feeling how the boy was trying to control her. He told her not to go to the class where everyone stretched, not when other men could look at her stretched out in front of them. She went anyways. He told her he wouldn't hand her the one thing they were all smoking when they handed it around to each other. She asked for it anyways. He told his friends they couldn't give her the other thing they all smoked in packs when she wanted one of them. That's when the girl snapped. She told him, straight out, to stop telling her how to live her life.

He told her he was sorry; he only wanted what was good for her because he cared about her. She wasn't seeing how this had all happened before, back in her life with the broken boy, but she had learned something from that time,

## WHO BROKE THE GIRL?

even if she didn't know where it was coming from. The girl wouldn't stop speaking up for herself. She told him she had gotten this far in life on her own and could make her own decisions. Then her sight clouded over. She couldn't see what he was doing later that night when he told her not to reply and to never repeat what he was about to say. He took control of the moment, and she never realized he was still trying to control her when he spoke the words – "I love you." The girl listened, didn't speak, and believed him. She still didn't know that this wasn't love, and what it was wasn't any good for her.

Then the week ended, and they ended, but she didn't want her happiness to end. The girl, who knew how to change, told herself she'd go as far as changing where she lived to keep it from ending. She was good at dreaming up a new life that would be difficult to live, and this one would have taken her further from her own life than she had ever gone before. His people all shared the same faith and to live among them one had to be the same as them. She already knew that, but his one friend reminded her on the drive to catch their flights. She wouldn't have mattered to anyone that lived where he came from, and could only matter to him for the one week he was away from that faith.

She still hadn't learned to see what wasn't good for her before giving herself over to what she thought would make her happy. This time she got lucky and wasn't given the choice that she would have made badly. The boy who had feelings for her knew their feelings weren't enough to give their lives over to them. The boy left and the girl didn't have to leave anything behind for him. She left his feelings behind by the water, where they had lived their short time together, and moved on to the city where her friend would meet back up.

WHO BROKE THE GIRL?

## BETTING AND BOUNCING

It took their next stay in a hectic city, followed by a stop next to the calmest water, before the tension between the two girls settled down. They found time they enjoyed in both, in-between multiple pops of tension. They tried to talk about it once but quickly turned away from what they couldn't see the same way. The girl, who hadn't said she was sorry, wasn't sorry. She knew anyone else would have done what she did, whatever they wanted to do, and she had enjoyed having done something for herself.

The way they'd parted wasn't the only thing that needed to be settled. The friend, who had just left him, was missing her boy even more than before. The girl felt her pain, but on the first day back together told her to snap back into this life they'd gone back to wandering through. The friends kept going. They left the tension hidden between them, and it would come back up whenever it reached a point where it couldn't stay down. When they felt it coming on they would step apart for a few hours and try to give the tension the space it needed to breathe itself out.

They made two stops in the next country they popped up to see. The first one brought the friend's sister, who brought her two little girls to celebrate their winter holiday. The girls splashed out more there than anywhere else and relaxed in a room as clean as the bright flat they had once shared. The girl was happy playing games, in and out of the water, with the sister's two girls. She played one little game everywhere they went with them, every day. She bet them to get them to do whatever it was they needed them to. She bet them to get them to eat more, to walk faster, to jump farther and to smile wider. After all the little games were over, the littlest one told her – "You're my auntie now too." The girl, who still didn't think she'd have her own little girl, had her feelings touched by this one.

In this clean place, with someone else's family, the girl made a decision that she was betting would make her happy for longer. After this trip spent wandering, she would move back to live in the country she had come from. She knew she couldn't go back and live in the new-old city, not after nearly killing herself there. She wanted to stay far away from both the work and the man that had almost taken all of

## WHO BROKE THE GIRL?

her light, she wanted more than that life had to give her. She had friends and family where she'd come from, and she wanted to be closer to them. So she decided it was time to take her energy back to the city that always had the most energy for her. She would make this trip her last wander, and bring her energy back to her city.

Right when she decided what her next life would be, she saw a public note, posted on her wall, from a man she had friended back when they worked together in that city. The girl, who had forgotten about this man, gave a public reply back to his note. Then they exchanged a few private notes about where the girl was. They left it with a bet he made her. If she took herself back, he would take her for a drink. They left it with that, they would say hello again after she moved back to the city where they would both be living. It would have been better if they had left it until then, but she would come back to him sooner than she should have.

Before that, the sister and her girls came with them to a second stop in this one country, but they didn't stay as long as the two friends. The girl stopped all her happy bets with the little girls and said a sad goodbye to them. Then the friends went out to say goodbye to the year that was ending and celebrate what was ahead of them. They met up with a girl the fourth friend knew from the new-old city, a friend who had come there with a group of strangers she was touring with. That night the girl saw how much her friend liked to put on a good show that got her a lot of attention. She saw that when her friend got it from this other girl, she didn't have that much to give her and didn't need that much from her. The girl felt herself get pushed over to second by the friend whose pain she had felt every day of the two months behind them. She didn't come in first on the night the girl wanted to celebrate with the only friend she had there.

The girl didn't remember it that night, but this had happened on another night. One that ended a year spent with the broken boy. She hadn't gotten any attention from the one she was with that night either. The broken boy had put on one of his shows for two girls who were strangers, and he was too wrapped up in the attention he was getting to stop and give her any. When she asked him for some, he told her – "It should make you happy to see other girls talk to me." She stayed quiet so there wouldn't be a fight on a night made to celebrate. It would have made her happy to celebrate the night with him, but it wasn't her happiness he cared about.

She didn't know on this night now that her feelings from then were coming back up. She should have been able to have her own fun with the nice strangers that were with them. But she hadn't stopped running between fun and work long enough to clear out the broken pieces she was still carrying around inside of her, the ones that kept tripping her. All she knew that night was that she didn't like feeling this way. The girl tried to stay quiet, but her feelings wouldn't stop coming up to hit her. The two girls fought quietly, and then the girl ran off. Without knowing where

## WHO BROKE THE GIRL?

she was going, she ran straight into streets crowded with other people's happiness. Somehow, the friend that was visiting from the new-old city found her and brought her back to celebrate the night with them. The two friends that were traveling together wouldn't fight again, not until the night before the day that would be their last one together.

For now, they turned their backs on their fight along with the crowds of this country the very next morning. The next to last country they ran through, before their next and last fight, was a good one. They went where the girl was most afraid to go, where she thought the people would hate her as soon as they heard her. All she knew about this place was what she had been told about the war her country had fought there, the one they'd lost. Those stories hadn't told her the truth about these people who she found to be nicer than anyone had been, in any country they had wandered through. The life there had an energy that felt like a good force, and she would never have understood it if she hadn't felt it herself.

It had the same good energy that she'd always felt when she was in her city, the one that gave her the most energy. She felt more energy there than in any other city she had ever been in, other than that one. She felt the energy coming from the people who had eyes that always smiled, even when their lips were straight. She felt the energy coming off the streets full of bikes that never stopped moving, that just flowed around them when they stepped out to cross in front of them.

Every one of the four spots they ran through in that country flowed with the energy the girl hadn't known she would feel there. The energy that she hadn't known she needed streamed in and ran through her. The friends started to feel like good friends again while there. They shared that energy, and her friend shared her feelings. Her energy was still going flat because of her boy, who was paying her less and less attention. She had been expecting this from the day she left, and what she had expected was what she was getting. The girl listened to everything and told her to talk as much as she needed to, however long it took to get this flat energy out of her.

During all this talking they wandered farther north and the cold they started feeling drove them away from this country's good energy. They decided they needed to feel more shine by resting next to the water. So they ran to a new spot, back in the last country they'd been in, which would be the last country they'd go to together. They went back to where things between them had gotten bad, not expecting that energy to still be there. They didn't know this would be their last run together when they left for the spot where the energy in their friendship would fully flatten.

Leading up to that the friend kept going flatter, and they were talking more about all the sadness she was feeling. The girl knew what this much sadness felt like, and she knew it wouldn't help to tell her friend not to feel what she felt. She believed the only thing to do when you felt that sad was to feel it all out. So she held space for her, so she would feel safe talking about it. The girl didn't think about what she was getting out of listening. It made her feel good to care for a friend who needed her; it made her feel like she was good and that she mattered. She needed that.

Then the friend who felt bad made the girl feel as bad as she felt. It happened the first night in the second spot they went to in that last country. Where they went because the fourth friend said she needed to have fun with other people that were like them. It was a spot that was hard to reach. They spent a whole day getting there. They carried their packs over their heads to walk out in the water to the small boat that rowed them to the small island that they then walked their packs across on their backs so they could then carry them up more short steps than could be counted. They were worn out by all the work they had put in to get there, but the two girls didn't rest once they got there.

They quickly cleaned up and went out to look for the good time that they had worked so hard to find. That's when they met the group that was having the loudest fun. It was full of guys and girls that looked like they were having the exact kind of fun that they wanted to be having. The kind they hadn't seen anyone having since the last night of the last year. This night there was one guy in this group that started talking to both of them, before he turned all his attention over to the girl. She knew he wasn't a guy she would like, but she liked the attention she was getting. She hadn't gotten any since she had put the boy who let her touch his feelings behind her. The girl enjoyed being looked at first again. The friend, who wasn't getting any attention, decided she wasn't having any fun, so she left them.

The girl chose to follow her away from everyone that was still having fun. She knew her friend was upset about her boy back home, but she didn't think she should be upset with her because of this boy. The friend's sadness sobbed up and cried out that she wanted to go back to her boy. The girl listened to her that night, then the next morning she left her to sleep it off and went to find the boy. She told him right away that she couldn't go have fun with him and his fun group of friends that day. They were going off to have an adventure, doing something she had never done before and had always wanted to, but she wouldn't do something that she didn't believe in. She wouldn't leave her friend sad and alone.

When her friend came to find the girl later that day, she told her right away – "I won't let you do this to me again." The girl couldn't make sense of the words her friend was speaking. She tried to understand, and then she tried to make her friend understand. She hadn't left her alone for that boy back then, and she wasn't leaving her alone for this boy now. The girl could feel her friend putting her sadness onto her, and she didn't want to take it. The friend, who she had wanted to help, was making her feel bad to make herself feel better. The girl got quiet under the weight of this sadness she had known so many times before and didn't want to feel again. She didn't speak for the rest of that day.

## SHARING TIME ALONE

The next day her fourth friend left her to go off on her own. The girl was left alone with the sadness she was now feeling. The safety she'd felt, being one of two on a shared wander, had left her. In a cabin surrounded by a dark forest, she spent the next three weeks sleepless with the fear that came from all the noises she heard in the darkness that surrounded her. She felt trapped in fear. Alone at the top of so many stairs, surrounded by too many trees, she thought about what could be coming at her from any direction. Every sound froze her. The freedom she'd felt the last three months was gone before the time to go back had come up.

## CRISTINA COSTANTINO

She spent some of her time in those days left, that now carried nothing but shine from above, with people that were staying near her, but she chose to spend most of it without anyone around her. The guy who had paid attention to her first stuck to her a little, but she brushed him off her. He still wasn't someone she could ever like. Then three nice boys asked her to teach them the card game they saw her playing on her own. These nice boys who were from a nice country where everyone was thoughtful to each other were nice to her. She had a nice time across a few days having thoughtful discussions with these three.

But the girl chose to spend most of her time alone with her thoughts. Facing the brightness that wouldn't stop shining on her, she quietly looked out over the water in front of her and thought back over the life that was behind her. Her thoughts didn't go anywhere they hadn't gone before. She still thought her work was the only thing that was killing her. She knew the man dying in his own life had been bad for her, but she thought he had only come into her life because of how close she had come to working herself to death. She didn't spend any of this time thinking about why she needed to work that much, so much.

She believed she had wandered and rested enough to leave the hard work her life had become, in the new-old city, behind her. She still wasn't thinking back far enough to see clearly and change enough to change her life. She still wasn't seeing the lessons she'd learned too young that were leading her life everywhere. She still wasn't seeing what had been broken even deeper while living with the broken boy. All the things she was still running from. Everything that drove her life to be hard work no matter how many times she drove herself to change where she was living.

Then she stopped thinking about herself, after barely starting, and distracted herself with something new she was doing. She had started writing to the man she was going to see when she moved back to her next life. The one who had bet her on whether or not she'd come back. She didn't know this man enough to know if she should like him, but she knew she liked writing him. She knew he looked like the kind of man she wanted to like. He had a strong look and a long history creating beautiful stories for work. A man with his history inked on his strong arms.

This man spoke to her in long notes, full of his long thoughts, during her long mornings facing the shine. His thoughts would arrive with her morning coffee, to be read by her while he slept through his night. Her reply back was there by his morning. Slowly, they started open each other up. She couldn't see that the distance between them gave her enough space to make her feel safe enough to open up to him. Safe enough to let him into her life without the fear that she would have to give her life over to him. She couldn't see that there was enough space there to keep him safe from having to give her the life he didn't have to give her.

The notes they penned were as friends at first. They even called each other pals. His notes told her about the one life he'd lived in the one city that had all the energy she loved. Her long notes back mentioned the lives she'd lived across so many different cities. Then he sent a note to tell her he was sad. He had lost the love of a woman he had thought was his to have for life. The girl felt sad for him. She could hear the truth in his words, but having started to care for him, she believed the words they shared were good enough to beat out his sadness. Her notes back told him the wisest words she knew about how to move on in life. She liked how it felt to help him, now that she didn't have her friend there to help. That's when his notes started to call her the thing she wanted most in her life. He started each with – "Good morning, sunshine."

That wasn't the only name he called her. They decided, together, to call each other by the names they had each gotten from the families they had felt hurt by. Two names, both hard to pronounce, that they liked calling each other. Their words never told, so neither ever knew, why they each felt hurt by them. What the girl knew was that she wanted to keep sending him sunshine and keep waking up to the shine he brought. She didn't know that he didn't have enough to keep this up for much longer.

What he could give her were questions, aimed to find out who the girl nowhere near him was on the inside. Each answer was followed by his answer to the same question, so she could learn what mattered to him. Then she would come back with her own question, to be answered by each of them. Their answers to all of these questions created a

## WHO BROKE THE GIRL?

cycle of words that filled out an outline of them. All his answers to all these questions felt wrong to her, but she would look at them and then quickly look past them, turning to fill in her own answers. If she had looked for longer she would have seen, this man saw life through eyes that didn't see what she saw. The materials that spoke out to him weren't the same as the thoughts she cherished. His belief in the work he created was waning, no match for the dream she still had for creating beautiful work that she could believe in.

This man, who had lost his love, liked the loveliness that was coming from her. The girl, who was losing her dream, needed a new one to believe in, and she liked the look of this one. The truth was always behind the words he told her. It would take him a while longer to take back his life from this other woman that he still loved. Despite that, a hope started to grow between them. A hope of what could come once the memory of this other woman faded. Even with all his wrong answers the girl let that hope grow. She gave him all the answers that were right for her, and she gave him hope for something that might be right for his life. Then she gave him something that wasn't good for her to give. She started to give her heart over to him.

During this time the girl got one answer that was what she needed and was so right for her. She wrote a note to her friend who had always been able to see her. She let her know she was coming back to the city with all the right kind of energy for her. The girl, who still had a hard time asking for help, asked to live with her at first. The friend, who had kept building a good life in that city while the girl had been out wandering, lived with the man she'd married. They had room for the girl to live while she got her life there started. The answer her friend quickly gave, to the question that was hard to ask, made the girl shine bright. There was no question she said – "OF COURSE!"

Those other answers, the wrong ones for her, came and went every day of those last weeks she spent living quietly under the shine and afraid through the dark. Then that time came to an end, and the girl was happy to go back and close out her life in the new-old city, the one that was already packed up and ready to be taken back. She didn't have to go back for long, but she wanted to stay there long enough to say a final goodbye to the dream she'd lived there. She decided it would be good for the man who had all the wrong answers to come see her there, so they could say their first hello in person. He decided she was right and said he would come.

WHO BROKE THE GIRL?

☆
## SAYING HELLO TO SAY GOODBYE

The girl went back to the new-old city where she no longer had a home or work to go to and all her things were ready to go. She stayed with a friend who she hadn't been close enough to before, that she would become closer to now, and would for a time stay close to even though she wouldn't live close to her again. She spent time with her third friend who still lived there even though she wasn't sure where she wanted to live anymore. While the girl had been gone she'd packed up her life and sent it down to the bottom of the world, to the country where she was from. After the girl would leave she would follow her things down, then bring them back up quickly so she could keep living the life she loved in the new-old city. They weren't as close now since they hadn't been living close, and they wouldn't be able to stay close after this short time back together.

The girl spent a lot of her time walking all the roads of the new-old city she'd gotten to know, roads she had almost called home for a lot longer, roads that she wasn't going to know for much longer. She spent a little time, one night, with the man who had tried to take her into the grey when they were both dying. While saying this final goodbye to the life she hadn't been able to live in the shadows, she spent the whole time looking away from him and down at the new life that was buzzing. Questions from the man she saw as her next life kept popping up. The dying man, who had always tried to convince her before, was being her friend again and left her to look forward to her new life.

During all of this time spent walking, and all of her time spent saying goodbye, her next life kept speaking to her. Making it easier for the girl to say goodbye to this one. The man with the wrong answers had all the right words for her at every moment. Their words shared more hope for them now, and they never stopped coming now that they had closed up some of the space between them. When they weren't writing their words of hope they were speaking them. Their first call, when she first got back, had started off with a quiver, but had grown strong over the six hours it lasted. They shared words every way they could about how much more they wanted to share as soon as they could.

## WHO BROKE THE GIRL?

Right after she got back, she heard from the friend she had wandered with, who had wandered away from her. Her fourth friend had found her energy and had found her way back home. The girl didn't feel good talking to her now, but she didn't feel right leaving without saying a friendly goodbye. She knew they would never see each other again to say one. They exchanged notes to try to make up for what had happened, but they both still said words that couldn't be understood by the other. The girl, who had been hurt when she was left alone, couldn't open up to this friend again, but she left the door to their friendship open. She invited her to come say goodbye to her when a few would gather for her last goodbye.

At the end of this long walk through her goodbyes, the man who had answered yes came over to say hello. Over a long weekend they said hello to the life they hoped to start together. He wanted her to come quickly, after he spent a short time settling in, so she rushed and came to him too quick for her own good. When he opened his door her eyes showed him just how wide open and hopeful she was on the inside. He wrapped his strong arms with all of their ink around her, and the girl felt safe with him.

They spent the next few days wandering with their arms wrapped around each other. They walked all the roads of the new-old city she was leaving, that she could barely find her way around anymore. They met up with old friends of his who happened to be visiting the city she would soon be leaving. One of these friends looked straight at them and said – "These two really like each other." She thought they did.

He stood behind her all night on the night of her last goodbye. The night where her only happiness came because of him and the friend she was staying with. The night her third friend came and left quickly, without ever getting too close to her. The night her fourth friend flattened her, again, when she wrote a short note saying she wouldn't be coming. The night the girl saw so clearly how little there had been to that life she had lived there. This all made the girl sad. She turned to him, looking to the life she was going to, to stop her sadness. He wrapped his strength around her, and told her exactly what she needed to hear – "I'll take care of you now." Then he said what she thought was their truth when he told her – "I don't know how we're going to get there, but I know where we're going." She was hearing what she had always hoped to hear from someone. She was worth it, to him, to push through the bad to get to the good.

If she had opened her eyes wide enough she would have seen how much they both wanted each other. Too much. She would have felt how tight their arms held on to each other. Too tight. She would have heard how hard he wanted to make it work. Too hard. The girl wasn't letting herself see how sad the eyes that were looking at her really were. She wasn't letting herself feel how his heart, that was too full of sadness, didn't have any room to be happy with her. The girl had come along when this man needed her, too early for her own good.

Even if she had come at the right time for him, this man would have been the wrong one for her. She could have seen it if she had looked close enough at how they were together. The need for each other was there, but there was no common ground underneath them. They were only right when having each other helped them both let go of something else. The right thing to do would have been to let go of each other before someone got hurt.

Only, she had given herself over to this dream already, and she was the girl who didn't want to stop dreaming. She couldn't see that she had only had this dream because it could never be more. Having this dream of a life with this man, who she couldn't really have, meant she would never have to give him her life. It was her safe way to dream. With a man who was good but still had hard work to do before he could be happy with anyone. She couldn't see that he was just like her.

Their long weekend wrapped together came to its end quickly. The man with all the wrong answers went back to where she would arrive soon enough. The girl said goodbye on the last day of that long weekend. Saying this goodbye didn't make her feel sad, somehow, she knew somewhere inside that this man couldn't make her happy for much longer than a weekend. She wouldn't come to believe in what she already knew until she tried, too hard, to make him believe in what wasn't true.

CRISTINA COSTANTINO

WHO BROKE THE GIRL?

☆

PART THREE

# WHEN THE GIRL RAN STILL

(YEARS: 34 - 37)

CRISTINA COSTANTINO

WHO BROKE THE GIRL?

☆
## HOLDING HER DREAM TOO TIGHT

As soon as she landed she started to feel different and was floored by what she was feeling. Her city didn't feel like hers anymore, and she didn't feel like herself. The jump back to a different life had shocked her thoughts straight out of her, again. She found that she couldn't find her way around the streets she had missed so much. She could understand what everyone was saying, but she couldn't stand how loud everyone was speaking. She could barely force a smile, that didn't feel right when it came, and she couldn't laugh with everyone when they laughed at things she didn't think were funny. Nothing sounded as clever as what she had just left behind. She was sure that she would never laugh again, and she couldn't believe that her dream to live a different kind of life had ended.

With no words in her head, her eyes started to open wider. She saw what she couldn't have seen before she got there. The city that had been hurt, first by other people and then by its own, was hurting too much to welcome her. The city that had once handed out dreams to anyone who came to it had closed itself up tight. The man, who had been hurt by his love, had been hurt more than she knew. The man she had felt close to had closed up tight, and she didn't know him now. He had no words for the girl, not now that she was in the city where he had lived a life with someone else. Back where he could only look back and could no longer see where they were going, like he had seen it before. Back where there was no space between them, there was no room for her.

She felt the truth on her first walk down his long hallway, to knock on the door that was closed to her. She felt in that moment how wrong this felt. She was headed towards a life that didn't feel like hers, but she pushed her feelings down and kept moving forward on the path she had already put herself on. She didn't turn around and head back, even though nothing felt right. The girl held on tight, trying to make everything fit like it had when he'd held her tight before.

Even though this felt wrong, she still had feelings for him, and at first it felt like they were growing. They still wanted each other, too much, just not in a way that could ever be enough. They couldn't push out the energy lingering from his past, it lay between them in his home that she didn't fit in and that didn't fit her. He told her his close friends couldn't know the truth about her, even though he wanted her to know them the second she got there. The friends that had known him with the woman before her would know how wrong it was that he was with her too soon after. So he needed them to think that she didn't matter all that much.

The girl knew she didn't want to know his friends so soon, not before they got to know each other better. She would have to see, through them, that she wasn't the right thing for him. She didn't listen to the voice inside of her, she did what he wanted, and she saw the truth quickly. Their eyes told her everything that was wrong about them. She sensed what they knew, that she wouldn't be in their lives long enough for them to have to bother getting to know her. The girl, who had been shocked into silence, couldn't even try to break down the walls they had up against her. She could only feel, even more, how she didn't fit in this life.

The girl, who was used to goodbyes by now, couldn't say goodbye to another dream, and she wouldn't let herself believe that she had to. She had started believing that she could make anything she dreamed up happen. She'd made the dream she had once wished on when she was little, to live back there, come true. Then she had turned her life into a new dream and made her move over to the new-old city. After that she had found the dream she had never even thought of dreaming up and had wandered straight through that one. So she had come back believing she had it in her to make any dream come true. Even one that wasn't right for her. She wanted more than anything to make her dreams come true, back in her city that had always had her energy, with the man she had dreamed up and surrounded by the friends she had always known.

Only, believing in something that was wrong wasn't going to make it right. Her belief in him started to go out the night they spent in his home with the friends who knew she didn't belong there. The man flinched, as soon as the night started, when she looked for him to give her some of his attention, and the girl looked straight into her past. Her whole focus shifted. What she saw in front of her looked just like the broken life she had already had with the broken boy. She couldn't look away and she couldn't look up, later, when he tried to throw her a quick look. She felt fear, knowing that if she looked she would see him; the broken boy from her past would be looking straight down at her.

That night wasn't a good time for her, and there wouldn't be any more good times for them. They still wanted each other too much, but that's all they had left between them. All the words that had once been written couldn't be spoken now. Their time, the one he had known they were going to get to, wasn't coming. The girl started to lose time while with him. She looked down one night, and when she looked up she couldn't remember the time they had just shared, the time that had passed.

## WHO BROKE THE GIRL?

The girl knew what she had to do. The voice inside her wouldn't let her live a life full of all the wrong answers, not again. It pushed her to push him out of her life. They pushed each other, but not hard enough. Not until he asked her a question one day in a note. A simple question asked about the night ahead of them. She answered that she didn't think she should see him since it didn't feel right. He knew it wasn't right for either of them. He took her answer about that night and used it to end them. He had half of the right answer. He knew they couldn't be together now, but he left the door open a crack for someday. He may have just been trying to soften the blow or maybe it felt safer to have a way back in. Either way, the whole right answer would have been to let it all go.

His words made the girl's fear come up quickly, and her mind started shouting all the wrong answers. She feared the loss of the hope she had held so briefly and could see the pain that was coming to replace it. Her fear pushed out the feelings that had been right. She couldn't see that this could never have grown into real love. He was only a trial run. Doing everything wrong with him would help her do more that was right later. She didn't know that then so she could only do what she knew, and she tried, too hard, to hold on to what wasn't right for either of them.

With her pain clutching her heart, she found her safe spot in second and decided to be his friend while his past came first. She still hadn't learned to not stick to something that was wrong just because she had once thought it was right. She told herself it didn't matter that she didn't matter to him now, she thought she could matter later, but only if she stayed in his life from now until then. She still hadn't learned how to go off on her own and make herself matter. What she would learn through this was that it was better to leave something alone when it wasn't right in that moment. But she didn't do that with him. Instead, they turned into two friends who would never be more, but could never be actual friends.

She kept pretending for a while that she could be a friend to the man who was wrong for her. They acted like friends who sent each other notes, again. Notes she sent wise words in, wanting to help him through his sad time, not seeing that she really wanted to keep herself from the sadness of losing something else. Notes she used to ask for his help in her search for the work she was finding out would be hard to find. They became friends who met for drinks and shared words about the lives they were no longer talking about sharing. Too often, these drinks turned into overnights that they shared. Nights she thought she was getting the love she wanted from him. Nights he was getting the only kind of love he still wanted from her.

Every one of those nights started off with friendly drinks. But after a few of them the man would shift to speak words about the nights they had once shared. He liked to remember them. The girl, who knew she still wanted to be more to him, knew how to be just friends. She pushed away those words, but he kept pushing them forward. He would open the door a crack with those words, and she would turn to look away. Then he'd pull her closer with more words until her words came out to meet his, and she'd tried to push through. Just to have him slam the door closed on her.

On these nights he never told her words that weren't his truth. He always reminded her – "I told you the truth from the beginning." He seemed to have forgotten all the other words he had said that had sounded true when she'd heard them. She hadn't forgotten. He was right that she had heard his truth, but he had never known hers. She was the girl who had learned how to have hope even when everything looked hopeless. Who had learned to wait through the hard times for her time to come, and who still wanted to believe that their time could come. She would hear his truth on those nights and add the hope she needed to keep her life going, then go back through the only door he would open for her now.

CRISTINA COSTANTINO

## OPENING OTHER DOORS

The girl spent her time, in-between these drinks, trying to open the right doors. She tried harder than she'd ever had to try before to find work. Working hard to find a place that would let her work hard for them was hard on her. She had always known she would have to put in a lot of hours once she found work, but she hadn't expected to have to put in so many hours across days that turned into three months to find that work.

She knew she was asking a lot from the city that had been hit hard. The place she wanted couldn't be too big or too cold, and they had to do beautiful work that its people believed in as much as she did. She knew she could help that place make great work, just like she had before. Only, it sounded like all of the work she'd done in the new-old city wasn't good enough for anyone since it hadn't been made here. She already knew the work she'd done here before, for places those in her line of work called below the line, didn't matter to those who worked above that line. She had enjoyed working below back then, but preferred working above, like she had over in the new-old city. She wanted to keep working up there now, so she kept pounding on the doors of those who did that here, asking to be seen by them.

She used all the energy she had, that wasn't being used up by her sadness over the man, to find the right answers for all the people she met. Seeing her hard work had always made her feel like she mattered before, and now that she couldn't find one she was having a hard time looking at herself. She couldn't believe how the city she loved and had chosen to come back to was making her work so hard to break back in. She had come back believing everything would be different and her life would be easier, but all she had changed was where she was living.

She pounded those city streets and felt like she was being pounded the whole time. She tried hard not to make the two whose home she was sharing see the heavy weight she was carrying. It didn't work. The friend who could see her saw how hard this was on her every day she lived there without finding work. She told the girl that this was how hard it was for everyone now. Her friend's husband, who was super social, was working hard to build up his own work using his skills at convincing people. He tried to use those skills to convince her to keep herself positive. She knew they were right, but it was hard for her to live this kind of life.

She told herself she didn't have it as hard as most even though she was going through a hard time. Then her worries got to her. The money she'd set aside to re-start a life after her wander could only see her through the little time she'd thought it would take to find work. Her family, who didn't have a lot, gave her enough to see her through a little longer. Then, she had to split her pride and ask her friend if she could give her the rest of what she owed her to live there after she found work. The friend, who had never wanted as much as the girl was giving her, said – "Of course."

The girl could have found low-end work to help her through, but that would have made her feel too low and would have split her pride even further. Instead, when she wasn't spending her time looking for work she made up work for herself. She started to read whatever she could pick up to push her mind to think smarter. When she wasn't thinking smarter, she was getting fitter. She ran all the cobbled roads around her friend's home every day that she lived there. If she wasn't running than she was swinging weights to get fit with her friend's husband, who told her what to do to make herself stronger. The girl worked hard at whatever would make her better so that even without work she could feel better. Then, just when she was fully spent and thought she'd have to run back to the new-old city that she knew had plenty of work waiting, her city decided she had put in enough hard work. It opened up for her overnight.

She had one long meeting that flowed across talks with four good people who talked about how good their work was and liked everything she said back to them about how she worked. She left knowing she had a good shot at getting the position. That was quickly followed by a talk with the lovable man in charge when he came back from being off. When they met he only asked questions about where she had wandered, but she didn't think twice and didn't care that he didn't seem to care about how she worked. She gave all the right answers and he liked what she told him. She liked what she heard when he said – "We're all nice to each other here." She knew this was the place she'd hoped to work.

She directed all of her positive energy towards the lovable man while she sat there that day. Then, that night, she willed her energy to drive him to hire her to do their work. She had waited long enough for her next dream to come along, and she wanted this to be that one. The next morning she got the note that said her energy had worked. Getting everything she wanted, she started working her dream the next day.

Now that the girl had found work, she got right to work finding her own place to live. Her friend's home was big, but they needed their space, and she wanted her own. In all the years she'd moved around alone she'd never lived on her own. She'd never wanted to. Being alone had always brought her sadness and at night had always scared her. She was afraid it still would. One of her old sisters, whose friendship she had just re-opened, convinced her of what she already wanted by telling her – "By this age you have to experience living alone." This friend, who was good at mothering her, was right. The girl knew it was time to learn how to be alone and to stop being afraid of the dark.

Once she decided to live on her own she found a place quickly. The third apartment she saw in the one neighborhood she looked in was the perfect dream home for her. It was small, but not too small for her, only too small for more than one to ever live there. It was older so it had the character she wanted, but everything in it was newer so it was as clean as she needed. One of its long walls was made up of strong bricks and seeing that made her heart happy. She was sure all her old things would fit in her new home. Everything she had bought back in the new-old city had been loaded up, carried over, and stored for her. Waiting for her to be ready with a new space. She moved in and quickly unpacked everything, carrying the energy from her last space into this one.

She loved how everything looked in the one way she saw to set it all up. Never even thinking to look for another way, one that would be a better way to live. The girl couldn't see how cold and unlived in she had made her space look. Everything she had to live on was pressed back against the walls, with all their hard angles coming out to meet her. If someone came over they had to quickly side step the travelling trunks she'd settled too close to the door. Once that one barrier was passed there was nothing to stop anyone from moving straight through and deep into the heart of her life. There was one short half-wall that blocked the small area she gave herself to rest in at night, but that wasn't enough to stop anyone from crossing the line.

A few would cross it a few times each, but none would stay long enough for any to settle into her life. There were enough places for more than one to rest, but all faced the same long, hard brick wall. She wouldn't be there much for the next two years, since she would start right back up working too much, but when she was she found herself alone more than she had ever been in her life. Sitting and facing that wall while staring at the box that spoke to her, the one she used to make herself numb so she could rest her thoughts.

WHO BROKE THE GIRL?

## SELLING OFF HER DREAMS

Her new work selling people their happy dreams, that she believed was going to be her happiest dream yet, started out as a good one. The lovable man in charge put her in charge of their biggest work, that they all hoped would be their best. The four she had met with were as good as she'd thought, and everyone else there was as nice as the lovable man had told her they would be. She was in charge of two young girls who were as nice and fresh as her hopes for this work. She loved those two more than anyone she had ever led before and wanted to do everything she could to keep them from getting spoiled.

She loved going to this work, and everyone there loved working with each other. What they were doing was good, and so was the group paying them to do it for them. The hours didn't run late so the girl could balance her work and her life. The people who paid them loved them and everyone would always hug after every meeting. More than she liked since touching at work made her uncomfortable, but she liked it more than if they'd been yelling at her to make the impossible happen for them. No one ever got angry with anyone at this work. The girl, who was used to being the one that took all the angry calls, couldn't believe her luck. She thought the long days of working late at night for people who wanted too much from her were finally behind her.

The place she worked had been really small when she'd started, but it quickly grew. Right after the girl got there a few new ones followed. They all had fun together at first. Every day while working they smiled across open tables at each other. The girl had found her happiness again, and near the end of the summer they all went off to celebrate each other. Everyone stopped working for one day and rode to a park together so they could ride a cyclone while they amused each other. It was the most fun the girl had ever had with any work. She wouldn't have believed it that day but soon after this work was going to spin her life upside down.

Now that she had the hope that this new work gave her, the girl could put the man with all the wrong answers

## WHO BROKE THE GIRL?

behind her. With this door that was now open she could stop trying to open the door to a life she wasn't supposed to have with him. She told him she had to shut down their friendship, that wasn't any good for her, and she stood by those words for a time after they were sent. She only opened it back up months later when she knew she could come back as just a friend. From then on they would be two people who met for drinks, and only that, once a year. The girl's feelings for him would linger for a while longer, but she refused to look at them, even when the man brought up the one thing they'd shared that satisfied him over those drinks. She'd given up on any door that led closer to him. Still, giving up on that dream, even though she now knew it wasn't the one for her, made her lose sight of the hope deep inside of her that had always kept her going. The girl stopped seeing her life through the rosy tint she'd always looked through and no longer believed she could make any dream happen.

After she left him behind, the dream that had come with this work started to break apart on her. That's when all hope disappeared from her life. They had won more work, which should have brought more hope, but it only brought the girl more work that was going to make her work a lot harder. Not too hard at first, but soon enough it would all be too hard on her. She went back to running between two streams of work. One that brought her up and one that dropped her low. Having missed worked for so long, she was happy to do it all again and didn't think about where it could lead or what it would do to her once she got there. She thought more work was good for her. It made her feel how much more she mattered there. The few months that had been quiet had been nice, but she'd worried throughout that they would think she wasn't working hard enough and decide they didn't need her. Fear had come up from inside to take her back over. She'd worked every day afraid it would be her last. The fear of not having any work to do again, and then not being able to pay for her life, had made her nerves too raw to touch. Her friend, who had seen her through the time she wasn't working, told her it was like she'd suffered a trauma and now had a disorder that caused her to stress more than she had to.

So she took on as much as they asked her to, and then did even more than they ever asked of her. She was doing what she knew. Working hard again made her feel good, at first. But she was about to get a hard push that would knock her back off-balance. One of the other new ones there was a man who was in charge of everyone creative, but since everything they did was creative he was really in charge of everyone, and he was going to change everything on them. For the first few months he was in charge everyone still loved everyone, until everyone worked for him a while longer. Everything started to go badly and it never stopped. The air around them grew tense, and everyone stopped loving this work, nearly overnight.

Through all this the lovable man in charge never asked about her work. He left her alone, and she knew she needed

## WHO BROKE THE GIRL?

to work like that so she liked it, but she also needed someone to talk to about what was hard. The people who paid them had changed themselves out. The new ones still hugged, but not all of them were as nice in between those hugs as the other ones had been. There was one new woman in charge of the group that paid them the most, and she had a need to control everything. The girl heard how careful she had to be of every word she spoke now, since one wrong word brought back a mean snap. The woman who now controlled them could instantly chill them with a cold silence, letting them know that nothing they did could ever be good enough for her.

In month-after-month of daily meetings this woman stared them down while putting them down. The girl took it the worst since she was the one paid to take it. She could never find the right words that would make this woman happy. The woman kept telling her to make the work they were bringing her better. The girl couldn't do that, and any words she said couldn't hide the truth since the woman was right about the work. It was impossible for the girl to fight this woman off by defending the work she knew wasn't good enough. Yet she couldn't tell the man in charge of the creative to change anything. He was the one paid to say what was good, not her, and he didn't want to hear what she thought about it. She still tried to tell him, using her softest words so she wouldn't anger him, and he always replied that he would make the changes the woman wanted, but then he never would. The girl, who believed in fighting for the team, went with him and the unchanged work week-after week to defend what she didn't believe in. She was working in a broken system.

By now everyone had seen how much she could do, and that no matter how much she did it was always good. That's when she started to feel she was being asked to do more than she should. The girl was doing twice as much work as anyone, and her two fresh faces couldn't help her, not as much as she needed. No one told her to stop, and no one ever would. She was the only one who could choose to stop, but she didn't know how to do that. Instead, she kept taking more on, and giving more of everything she knew how to give. She gave everything she had to the work that she loved too much for her own good, never seeing how much she loved it more than herself.

She thought she was the only one who could handle it, but trying to handle it when nothing she tried mattered was taking it out of her. Since she was leading the work the man in charge of the creative loved the most, she worked with him the most. This man could be scary, and he scared everyone at some point, but he scared the girl at most points. She felt her charge to protect her fresh faces from his scary one, so she always stood between them when those points came. She was stuck on the point of fear almost every day that she worked now. He did it to protect the work he loved but couldn't see how he was killing the place that everyone had loved working.

## WHO BROKE THE GIRL?

The girl, who still had too much fear stuck inside of her, felt her fear come up and overwhelm her every time he scared her. It was hard to explain why he scared her so much more than anyone, since she didn't know where her fear came from. He never raised his voice or threatened her straight out. He was a smart man who used his words wisely, but they held an energetic undertone, when he chose to place it, that felt like a dangerous threat was behind them.

Even if she hadn't had to work with him more than anyone else, his words would have still struck her harder. The girl knew his threat. She had felt it tense in the air around her across the first half of her life. Then she had chosen to let it choke the voice out of her. With every threat that he didn't speak loudly, the fear rose up inside of her and pushed hard to crack her.

The girl could have chosen to leave the energy that wasn't any good for her, but the fear that had overcome her when it took a while to find this work was harder to face than this silent threat was. So she lived with her fear, and beat it back the only way she had ever learned how. The girl, who was already working hard, started working harder.

She took on a lot while asking for a lot from the girls who worked for her, always thinking she was giving them a lot back. But all that she gave came with the weight of the fear that came on when the man scared her. She could have done better by them. Not being able to handle the fear that was hurting her, she started to lean on them more than she should have, more than they could handle. Trying to protect them but instead projecting her fear, she was letting his scare pass straight through her and hit them.

While cracking with fear she kept working hard, and fighting harder to protect the creative work. What she was doing worked for him, and he started to like the way she worked, so his words went off to threaten others more than her. He used his words to scare people when he thought their work wasn't good enough. The girl made sure that everything she did was good enough for him, and she started to feel less fear of him. She thought she had turned things around for herself by showing him how much the work mattered to her, which was all that mattered to him. But, she was just doing what she had done before, backing away from fear so it wouldn't hit her. While everyone else started to like him less, the girl started to like him more, since she didn't have to face how much he scared her any more.

The lovable man, who was still one of the two in charge, couldn't stop the other man from scaring them, but then he was never there to see him get scary, and it was hard for him to believe what he couldn't see. This man loved seeing everything that was good in life, and he didn't want to talk about anything bad. She loved how he saw things, but she didn't love that he couldn't see how the scary man and controlling woman were bad for all of them. This lovable man had a lot of love for his people at work, but even more for his people outside of work. She loved the love in him, but she didn't love that she no longer had

## WHO BROKE THE GIRL?

enough of her own time, outside of work, to find something else to love.

She started running from home to work because of how much work was piled on. She'd gone right back to working hard while running away from life. A life that she had tried to take back when she'd been out wandering, but had lost sight of after she'd lost the hope the wrong man and then this work had brought her. Her wandering had relaxed her, but it hadn't changed her. She was back living the same life as before, one given over to work. A life she made matter by showing how much she could work. So she started to work harder, to live a life that mattered even more. That's when she lost her balance again, and she started working herself back towards death.

The girl who needed her work had shown everyone around her how much they needed her to keep working. The woman who controlled them was demanding more from them. The man who was lovable was showing up less. The man who could be scary was threatening everyone more. The girl pushed herself more, instead of pushing back, and she started to fall over. The girls she meant to protect started buckling on her. She was doing it to herself all over again. The hours got longer, starting earlier and lasting later.

There was less and less time for the girl's life, so her work became her life. She'd started this work being called by the name she'd last been given, the one made up of her two broken initials, but she was starting to be known by even less, and she liked it. One initial that wasn't even hers became what the called her. It stood for the half of her name that sound like a boy, and marked the spot where she existed. They used this initial to call out to her, sometimes adding the second half of her name, the one that sounded like some other girl altogether. The girl she had started to find when she went off wandering was disappearing.

Then they had the big meeting where the woman who controlled them pointed her out in front of everyone. She blamed the girl for what she wasn't getting and said she wasn't doing enough so needed to work harder. The girl broke down inside and struggled to not let it all pour out in front of them. She knew there wasn't anything more she could do to give her what she wanted. Everyone there who was good knew the truth. After the meeting another woman who was high up came over to tell her she knew how much she was doing and that it was enough. This one was always good to her. The lovable man who happened to be there had now seen for himself how bad she could be, and he went above the controlling woman. He threatened her by talking to the man that was over her. Her need to control everything that wasn't controllable had beaten the girl down, but the lovable man beat her back.

☆
## ONE OF MANY

The first year back, with all that work that was dragging her down, was full of friends that were lifting her up. She made friends with the small team around her that was good to her, and she had good times with. The two young ones who had fresh faces. The one girl who made her laugh and had the girlfriend with the smile that was so wide it made everyone smile. The small girl who could make big things happen. The guy with a birthday the day after hers and the boyfriend whose birthday made him a lot younger. The two who started as partners who created work together, and then became close friends with sons born the same year. The tall one with the good heart who had the girlfriend who looked just like him. The one who knocked on the floor for her luck, that the girl would be lucky to become better friends with later. It was a small team full of good people.

By the time she worked with them she'd lost the way of speaking that made her sound like she was from an in-between world, but she still liked to laugh, just like she had with the people she worked with when she lived in that new-old city. She laughed with everyone on this small team while they worked hard, when they took a break, and then whenever they stopped for a few drinks after work. She wasn't drinking or laughing with this work as much as she had with her last, but she was still happier here than she had been there. They never became more than work friends, even though they sometimes saw each other outside of work, but they were all friends while they worked together.

Outside of work, she spent time with her sister-friend. They had stayed friendly across the years she was away, and the girl had always stayed with her when she'd come back for her short stays. Now that she'd closed up the space between where they lived, their lives grew closer. These two were different, but they had one thing in common. Both girls had separated themselves from their families, the ones they shared by the one marriage. The friend would drive them home for their short stays, to see these families, and they would always talk about how different they were from them and how much more alike their lives were to each other.

## WHO BROKE THE GIRL?

Back in the city, they spent their time together sitting in a big park talking about the prospects they had for the lives that had hurt them. The lives that they had created with all the choices they'd made. The lives they thought hadn't been as easy on them as life had been for others. The girl knew she didn't like to look at the bad that had happened in her life that much. She wanted to look past the bad and see the good that had come through it, so the two didn't spend too much time together.

The friend they used to share, the one who didn't give herself enough to live and hadn't wanted to let go of her at first, was still friends with her sister-friend. The girl didn't think she wanted to be friends with her again, but then changed that thought. She didn't think she could let go of what she felt had been done to her that last night before she'd left, but then she did. The friend who wanted her back didn't let pride stop her. She reached out to the girl, and she reached her, so they became friends again.

Their connection came back, even though they had less in common than before, and they grew close over what they still shared. The girl, who didn't give herself enough, gave her friends all of her loyalty and had more than enough to give. Both girls were good at giving that and at not giving themselves what they needed, in different ways but with the same lonely result. Neither one could find a love that treated them right. Both girls struggled with their work, in different ways but with the same tough result. Neither one could find the right work that gave them back what they needed. So they gave to each other and helped themselves by distracting one another. Their friendship was shadowed by all their struggles and it was a shadow of the friendship they'd had back when they used to have fun.

The girl who'd only had a few friends in the new-old city wanted more in this one. So she went back to the last work she'd had in this city to find another one. Not the one girl she'd been good friends with then, that grounded friend had already moved back to the city she came from. Instead, she closed in on another girl, one she'd only known a little back then, and they got a lot closer now that she was back to stay. This girl, who worked like she worked, knew the hardships of their work. She could talk to this girl who understood how hard it was when she couldn't find work and how hard work was once it was found. They were both thoughtful about their work and liked to help think through how it would make people think when they saw it, even though no one thought they should do that part of the work.

These two met up and talked a lot. They talked about being tired of how their role was the one no one thought mattered. They were both tired of being the one that got punched at work when anyone felt like giving someone a punch. They talked about how they didn't know if they could do this type of work much longer. The more they talked, the more they knew how much they had in common, so they saw each other more, but their friendship would have to take a break. This girl who worked like her moved

## WHO BROKE THE GIRL?

around like her. She met a boy she really liked who wanted to move, and since she was planning her own move they decided to go together. She left the city behind but once that didn't work out she'd come back, and they would go back to talking a lot.

After she stopped living with her friend, the one who could see her, she saw her less. They were never going to stop being friends again, but their days were too full of life and work to find more time for each other. When they did see each other they would talk with a lot of wisdom about life. Both worked hard and needed to rest hard. Their minds, that were both overworked, didn't want to think hard when they weren't working. So at times the two wouldn't talk when they met, instead they rested their minds together. Turning off their thoughts, all words were shushed, and they turned on the box that talked to them.

This friend wasn't the only friend who used to be her sister that she had in her life now. Some of those friends from then lived here now, and she wanted to make them into her good friends again. Across all the years lived across so much space the girl hadn't stayed close to them. She'd needed to see more before she could see them again. Now she wanted them back and knew it was time for them to see each other again.

She started with the friend who was so good at mothering her. The space between them had grown much smaller since her new home was only a few blocks away from hers. This new mother lived close by with her husband who had good energy and their son who was just one. The girl jumped to see her any time the mother called to say she had time that was free to share. The time they shared was good, but it would have been just as good if the girl hadn't jumped to make her time fit her friend's life. It would have been better if they found a good time that fit both of them.

This friend always listened and advised her in the time they spent walking around their little village, where they lived on the right side of everyone. The girl had always looked up to this one, now more than ever, so she always listened to her friend's words of advice. The words were wise, and it was good for her to listen, but the girl could have listened to her own wise thoughts and learned just as much. Only, it was easier for her to hear this mother's voice than it was to hear the voice inside of her. The one that had always been with her, and that she had only been able to hear when it spoke louder.

She loved watching this friend lovingly mother her son, always putting him first in life. The girl, who didn't think she'd ever have her own, wanted to stay close enough to watch this one across all the years it would take for him to grow up. Watching him instead of growing a child of her own felt safer. She didn't have to give her life over to one that wasn't hers, one that she didn't have to put first.

The girl closed up the space with another old sister. One she had loved to stay up with and listen to across their nights back in that white house with all its straight walls. This one was strong and had strong opinions that she always told straight. The girl listened to her opinions. Agreeing with a lot of them, the girl still listened to the ones that didn't sit right with her. When she didn't agree she would come back with her own opinion, but her strong friend always stood by hers and would come back to say them louder, so the girl always stopped her own. The girl who was still afraid of anything that came close to sounding like a yell still believed what she believed, but she couldn't push against her friend's strength. She still didn't have enough of her own to keep speaking out.

The girl loved the strength in her friend with all the opinions, and she loved watching her use her strength to take care of herself. She fell for boys, but she never let herself fall because of them. She chose ones that wanted her first, and then always kept herself in first with them. Whenever she realized that the one she had chosen wasn't the right one for her, she would make a strong decision and quickly let go of what wasn't right. The girl liked seeing how she put herself first.

This friend, despite her strong opinions, was like the girl in one way that was different. Both girls had lived different lives in different cities, and both had just moved back to this city where they were both building their new lives. Unlike the girl, this friend had always kept her old friends close and they were now close by in this city. The girl liked them and thought she could see herself being good friends in their group. She couldn't see that she was only like them a little and would only be around them a little.

## CRISTINA COSTANTINO

Their group didn't need more friends, and even though she thought she did, she didn't need a group. Instead, her and this friend would have one good friendship that was just between them.

She didn't get close to any others at this time. There would be time for a few new friends later, but these were the ones she kept close to her for now. They were the ones that mattered to her, even though she couldn't let herself see how much she mattered to them. These ones, who she liked so much, liked her just as much. She never could see that some of what she liked in them was in her too. She may have seen herself more clearly, sooner, if she had looked at them more closely.

A few of them were friends with each other, but none of them came together as one group of friends. The girl had lived past lives in a group, but she wouldn't have that in this life. She didn't know why this was the way things were since she thought that was what she wanted. She saw other groups out there looking happy together, and she was sure she would be happier in one. She tried to make it happen by bringing some of these friends, the ones who knew each other from before, together. Her friends were always happy to hang out, but the girl was only happy for a short while during these times together. She heard herself speak less when more people were there to be heard. She saw herself pull back from them even though she wanted to pull them all together. She felt invisible when more people were around her that could be seen. So instead of pulling together more, she spent more time one-on-one, running from one friend to another.

She felt safest when she was alone with any one of her old friends, but being one of only two now scared her. If she didn't have just one friend around her all the time then she wouldn't lose, even if she lost one again. If she didn't have one in front of her all the time, then she could stand out on her own, as herself. She started to get used to being one with a lot of space around her. One who ran between many that she wanted to keep close now.

There were times when the girl brought her friends together and felt both seen and heard. Not when she got together with those that knew each other, but when she brought two who weren't friends together. One summer she spent a lot of time with these two friends, out by the end of their world, to rest themselves by the water. The girl still worked herself hard during those weeks that were hot, but on a lot of the hottest ends of those weeks she rested just as hard. It took a lot of time to get out there, but once they were there they always had a good time together. The change in the air, that helped her ditch the strain that came from work, made the time spent getting there worth everything.

In the mornings the girl would jump out of the house they shared with strangers, to drink coffee made by a witch of a woman and stare out at the water filled with strangers who were floating while waiting for the next wave to lift them higher. The girl got out there early with her friend who had the strongest opinions. They shared their life stories and quickly got to know each other again, better than they had ever known each other before this time they now shared. They would share these stories while sharing opinions on how they wanted to live different from the way they had lived before.

After a few hours of this story time, her friend who hadn't given herself enough to live would join them. She wouldn't give herself any sun while sitting under the shade she brought with her, but she would give them her opinions. This one's opinions were just as strong as those of her other friend that she was just getting to know again. Sometimes they were the same, but the shade she put on her words was always different. This friend was hurting inside and it came out in the way she spoke her opinions. Her father, who she loved deeply, was disappearing deep inside of himself. She had to watch him disappear from her life slowly and it was turning into her own slow death.

These three would spend their whole day sitting in the sun-shade, then walk along the edge of the water to the town at the end of this world. These were happy walks filled with happy talks, followed by happy nights for the girl. The nights that came after these days were always late ones. They moved from bar to bar, to have one drink after another, and the girl went back to kissing one boy after the next. Boys whose names didn't matter. Boys she had fun with in the moment and could then forget right after. Boys who weren't men she might care about or who could bring up her pain and then leave her.

There was one boy she met that summer who she didn't have any fun with. She met him the first night out and they only talked for a moment. In that moment he decided he knew her better than she knew herself. He asked her where she was from, and she paused before answering, not knowing what the right answer was. She knew where she'd been born but it had never felt like where she was from, even more so now that she had lived in so many places. She knew he was trying to figure her out, but where she was from didn't define her. He jumped on her after her paused response, telling her he knew the place she'd been born and therefore knew her. She told him loudly that he didn't know what he was talking about. The girl didn't say more; she knew this one could never hear the truth in her words.

That was the only moment in all that time that didn't make the girl happy. She was back with old friends, and she was back where she felt the most balance, resting herself by the water. This was where she could always hold on to her balance. She was happy she chose to spend her time there, and wondered why she had never chosen to live her life by the water that calmed her. She knew this life would have been good to her, but she also knew it wasn't enough for her. The girl still needed the rush of a hard day's work to give her the high that she only knew how to get from something that wasn't good for her.

CRISTINA COSTANTINO

WHO BROKE THE GIRL?

☆
## BACK TO THE WAY THINGS WERE

The summer that was happy outside work came to an end quicker than she would have liked, and she went back to working her weeks without any rest between them. The girl knew her hard work wouldn't end any time soon, but she didn't know things at work were about to get even harder before an end came to that work. She went back to going to work early, just to run home late carrying her work with her so she could work even later. Her body kicked her to try to get her to stop heading towards this death she was marching straight towards. She felt its pain, but she couldn't stop. The work had to get done so it could get made before it was too late. She was sure if she stopped then nothing would get done.

So she never stopped. Instead, she pushed herself and everyone around her for the work that mattered so much to her. She knew if they didn't work harder then the woman who controlled them would put an end to them. The woman who was pushing them every day to see all the work she'd been waiting for them to redo right. Her boss pushed to know what they had done to make their work better, so it would be worth the money they were paying them. They had two meetings in one day to work up to, where they were going to have to prove their worth. The girl pushed everyone she worked with to work harder than they were to make these meetings turn out well for them.

She worked late the night before that day with the one creative who was working just as hard as her. Everyone who would be next to her in those meetings had already gone home to get their rest. She finally ran home so she could work into the early hours. On one hour's sleep she pulled the work together, in time to make the first morning meeting, followed by that afternoon's second meeting, the one that she would be running. Her body screamed at her to stop, but she couldn't stop long enough to listen. Those meetings had to work. She pushed it to make it through the first and to hold on through the long wait before the second. Then, while sitting in front of all the expectant faces in that second meeting her body started to lean itself over, trying to get her to stop by making her fall in front of everyone.

She didn't fall and they didn't fail. They got praise for all their work, and she got the high she needed. Everyone thanked her, but the best line she got came from the creative president above the creative man in charge. He'd seen what she'd gone home with the night before, and after the meeting he told her – "I don't know how you did it, but what you did made us all look good. Thank You." She didn't know how she did it either, especially when she felt too tired to do anything. She never stopped doing it all while she kept on pushing her life away from her. Any day off from work was now spent sleeping, not living. When she wasn't sleeping, she tried reading, but her tired mind wouldn't let her think for herself. Putting all books down, she tried to pick herself up with her friends, but all she could talk about was how work was dragging her down. The only thing she could see was the work. The girl couldn't see how she had done this all before, and that there was only one way it would end.

All that work done for those two meetings led to nothing but more work. What everyone had loved for a moment would never get made. Instead, they would have to work harder and faster to create new work to meet the same deadline that was now closer. The president over everyone had hated the creative idea. Even before that work started, other things started to come to an end. The man who was lovable had found new work and wouldn't be with them any longer. On his way out, he told her – "Find something you love outside of here." His words made her angry, she had too much work to do to find time for anything else. She didn't know she was the one letting this work take her life over. She hadn't protected herself when she'd started, hadn't pushed against what she'd already known wasn't good for her. She had done it to herself, again, so would have to repeat this lesson.

She wasn't the only one that had to learn a lesson. Right when the lovable man took his love away, one of the other workers decided he'd had enough of this place. On his way out he told the men high up what everyone thought about the one man left in charge. That's when they found out that he scared them. That drove those men come to work with them. They heard the same thing from everyone except the girl. She'd learned to live with that fear again, so she told them he didn't scare her. The work mattered to him and that was all that mattered to her. She couldn't see the fear that she'd accepted as a part of her life.

Things started to change quickly then. One of the men who had come, one who looked like a mad man, really wanted to help. He was smart and full of good power. He stomped his energy around and told everyone to work harder or get out. He saw her and liked how hard she worked, so he told her he would fix everything that was breaking down on her. The mad man thought he could make it a good place to work again. He was a good man and brought a good energy to their work.

## WHO BROKE THE GIRL?

The mad man and the scary man worked together at first, but he had already scared too many of them for this to keep working for much longer. She was working with him less, but still enough. Then she did what she'd never done. She pushed him on some work. He threw his threat at her with a finger he threw in her face. This time she knew she had the mad man behind her, and he would get mad for her. She felt that power, and she said loudly – "I'm not going back to when you talked to me like that before!" She didn't have to. He soon left them to their work and went to find a new one.

More people stopped working there, so more started. The girl kept feeling her power while things were changing. She had more than before, and more than enough now. The mad man, who spoke loudly, listened to her when she spoke. He asked her to speak more, so she started to speak even louder and started to feel like she was winning. She spoke out about what was breaking their work. He wanted to fix it, and she thought he could, but she would find out that she was the only one that could clear out what was broken in her life.

It didn't take long before the girl started to lose. First, she lost the fresh faces around her. One and then the other chose to leave. This work, and the way the girl worked it, had made them want to break free of it. She had tried to be good to them, and they had worked hard for her, but she had pushed them too hard. These girls didn't need to work themselves into the ground. It hurt the girl to say goodbye to them, so she didn't. On the last day each of them was there she let work pull her away, so she never had to say goodbye to their fresh faces.

The mad man was still stomping around, and he used his power to bring her new, fresh help before her old help ran out. That's when the girl got the best help she'd ever had. Two helpers who drove themselves as hard as she did came down to give the girl their best. The girl and these helpers made the best work out of one of her two streams. They made it all work throughout the storm that hit her city the hardest, not letting its flood stop their energy for even one minute. They had the best time doing a lot together, both in and out of work. The girl was thankful for these two, and she cooked them a big meal to give them all her thanks on the day everyone else was thankful for the families sat around them.

Another new helper, who had just started, came to that dinner with them. She had come down to take the place of one of the two who had only come to give her short-term help. So the girl lost one of her favorites. The girl liked this new one, almost as much as the other two, but this one wasn't going to help her. This one didn't want to just help. She had come down thinking she was taking charge of the work, but she could only do that by taking it away from her. The girl tried to give her what she wanted but it was hard for her to let go of how much she'd been doing, both for her and for the ones paying them, so she fought it.

## WHO BROKE THE GIRL?

Thanks to the mad man, the girl got to hire another girl to help her. She thought she could see herself in how strong this one looked, and she thought she was finally getting enough help with her work and wouldn't have to work so much of the time. Only, this one's help came with mistakes the girl had to clean up after, which forced her to work harder. She could have forgiven her for that, but she couldn't forgive this hire, that she had now decided was a mistake, for not owning her mistakes. The girl who thought she always saw her own couldn't stand to see this. She couldn't see herself to forgiving this helper, just like she could never forgive herself. Instead, she started to drive her harder, which drove her straight out of there. The girl was happy not to see her or her mistakes again.

Another man came around that time, to be one of the ones at the top. She thought this man's work would help her bring in more work. He was a smart man who could see things they couldn't see clearly, but he couldn't see what he was doing to her. He saw the old work that hadn't been good enough, that the girl hadn't been able to make better, and he slammed her for it. She heard the blame she'd already put on herself in how he spoke to her.

He tried hard to make the work better, but his work didn't make anything better. His frustration matched hers, and they became frustrated with each other. She pushed him to do more, when she couldn't do any more herself, and he pushed her straight over the edge when he wrote to everyone – "I'll do it, since you can't do your own work."

The girl, who knew how bad it felt to be out of work, started to feel like she couldn't work there one minute longer. She pushed herself to push this feeling away, and she kept pushing herself to work harder and harder.

The girl who was pushing was being pushed to work even harder by the woman who controlled her other stream of work. The work that had been shown, but never made, was still slated to be seen during the biggest game of the year, and it had to be more than super if it was going to save them. So they had to think up new work quickly, straight through that one hard storm, and then they had to get it made by working straight through the biggest holiday. When they came back from working that holiday there came a new man who would manage them closely. He came in to take over since the mad man had to go back where he'd come from. All of his stomping had drained his power, and he needed to take care of himself by working less. This new man who managed them closely could see how she worked as soon as he started, and he praised her. He pushed everyone to work harder, across more hours, but he didn't push her. He could see she was already working almost every hour, every day.

By now she was working twice as many hours, plus ten more, than one was meant to in one week. She wasn't the only one. Every week, week-after-week, everyone on her small core team worked themselves to death. Everyone worked to their breaking points, and then to the point that they would break with each other. The girl still didn't like the

## WHO BROKE THE GIRL?

work they were creating, but she had been told that what she thought about the work didn't matter, so she didn't voice her opinion. Everyone's hard work had been seen and liked by the woman who controlled them and everyone who controlled her. That was all that mattered. Everyone loved everyone, until the work they made was seen by the world, and no one loved it. Then no one who had worked so hard on it loved anyone anymore.

Working so hard for work she'd known wasn't good enough and hadn't been able to make better, but still had to stand by when everyone saw it wasn't any good, completely crushed her. The day after that work lost, after the weekend of non-stop work, she came to work feeling broken. She knew how she felt, but was too tired to care how she looked. The man managing everyone closely told her – "I've never seen anyone look so broken." He could see it, even though he didn't see her later, when her broken body lost control while she hid herself away to hide the shaking. Only coming back out when she could get some control back over it. Work hadn't stopped, so she couldn't stop, even though she could feel all the breaks inside of her widening. The girl's body went back to shouting at her to try to stop her. Her lungs pressed themselves in to keep her from taking any deep, calming breaths. Crushing the life out of her, and forcing her to take a long drag on what a doctor had given her to force her body to let her breath in.

Soon there wasn't any work left for her to breathe for. Everyone that held the power had decided. This work, that they hadn't been able to create better, would go away to be created by those who might do better. The girl wasn't told she was losing this work until just before everyone was told. She couldn't be told because there was one who was losing more. This one wouldn't be working with them any longer. The man who managed everything didn't have to tell her what she already knew, they didn't have enough work to keep her busy either. Not having any work for her to do mattered to her, but it didn't matter to them. They weren't going to let her go. They had seen her break herself for them, and they wanted to keep her for the next time they needed that. He told everyone the work was lost, and then what the girl needed everyone to know – "We would have lost this work eight months ago if it wasn't for her."

She may have been able to put the work that had landed so low behind her, if either she or the work could have risen up higher. She couldn't do less than she had been doing before, and she still needed to do beautiful work that she could believe in. Only, there wasn't any good work to do. They would have to win more, but the girl no longer believed this place could do that type of work. Then, the only work she had left to do, that wasn't enough for her anymore, was taken away from her.

The man who managed them closely had started to do some of her work. He was still new there, and needed to do that to get in with those that paid them. Instead of rising up, she felt pushed down. At the same time her helper, who wanted to be in charge, was pushing up on the same work.

## WHO BROKE THE GIRL?

So with the new man in charge pushing her down from above, and her new helper pushing up from below, she let herself get pushed straight out of there. They couldn't see what they were doing, and the man tried to keep her by reassuring her that he could change what wasn't working there, but they had already lost her.

The voice inside her spoke out loudly, and told her – "Enough". Enough of working hard on what she didn't believe in for people who took it away from her. It was time to give up on this dream that had dropped her. She'd been working too hard to look around too much for other work, but the girl had made a few calls. Only, she knew she wouldn't be able to do any work for a while. She had worked her mind and body too hard, and they wouldn't let her keep using them up this way. She needed to stay still and do nothing, so she decided to take a long summer break.

Before she could break off to do that, a place praised for their creative work called her. She couldn't say no to their call, even though she had nothing left to give. She went to talk to them on her last day of work. The two creative men who were in charge there asked her about what she'd worked on and why it'd left them. She told them the truth, even though she knew they wouldn't want to hear it from her. Sounding hopeless, she voiced what she knew, and said – "Our creative wasn't good enough." Before she left them one of the two said it was brave of her to leave one work without another. She told him another truth – "I had no choice. Doing work I didn't believe in was chipping away at my soul."

WHO BROKE THE GIRL?

☆
## TIME SPENT OUT OF WORK

The first day after her last, the girl was struck. With no work to her name, she wondered – "Who am I?" She didn't know, but she knew it was time to find out. Remembering the man in that book that had once helped her, before she was ready to help herself, she decided it was time to sit still, so she set out to find her own bench. The girl put herself to work trying to find the power inside of her, and she started a new routine that would be hers alone for the next few months.

Without seeing the parts that were still feeding the part of her that needed to work, she rose early every day, even though there was nowhere for her to run to. She opened up her days by watching what was being broadcasted about the world outside of her city. Then picked up the paper, that was full of words that told the deeper story behind what she'd heard, and brought it to her bench. Reading every word, from cover to-cover, every morning of every day that she sat on her bench, she felt satisfied. Thinking how good it was that she finally had time to open up her mind, not seeing the need she still had to keep working.

Then one day she put the paper down and sat completely still. While looking up, she felt the power the book had mentioned. She stared at the light shining down on her through the leaves of all the trees around her, and she didn't move for the longest moment, never wanting to stop looking up. All the beauty around her struck something deep inside her heart. She didn't have to do any work for this beauty that didn't ask anything of her and didn't take anything from her. It had already been created and was just waiting there for her to notice it. Feeling it shift her energy, she was overwhelmed by it and by the happiness she felt inside of her. It was a new high, one that took her higher than she'd ever been before and came from everything that was pure good in the life around her.

The girl started to change after the day she looked up; she was coming closer to waking up. She still took some time out to read the paper, but it had started to overwhelm her with so many words that spoke of so much death. She now chose to use her time sitting still for longer and just looking around at life. Surrounded by this beauty, she was starting to see that there was more to life than work. She

## WHO BROKE THE GIRL?

was finally feeling how much she mattered because she was alive, not because she could work. Not having work to go to stopped bothering her, and she wasn't sure she could start back up with the same one that had taken all hope away from her. Turning further away from death and looking up in wonder, she started to wonder if she could do good work that wouldn't kill her. She thought she knew something she could do that would make her feel good, the same thing that had always made her feel her goodness. The girl wanted to help people.

She spent some of her time considering how she could do that. Thinking about how much she wanted to help the ones she'd read about, those dying a world away, she spent time looking up what she could do for them. A new dream, one she had never had before, was trying to form, but she still couldn't let go of the last one that had once meant so much to her. Whatever she did, she still needed to be considered good at her work, and she had been good at that one. She knew that to do a new kind of work she would have to start all over again. Struggling with herself, she wondered if she could do that.

For the next few months, any time spent thinking about work was spent on thoughts of what the new one could be. No time was spent looking for the same kind of work that had taken her breath away from her. She didn't want any of her freedom to go towards anything that had to do with that. If someone called to talk about it, she would spend some of her time talking, but she refused to do any work to find someone to talk to her. Instead, she found a good way to keep moving in-between her stillness. She worked her body hard by running it next to the water that ran near her. She knew this kind of hard work was good for her since it leaned her body down and cleared her energy out. She lost the weight she'd been carrying when she was working too many hours to find one to take care of herself in. After the hours spent taking in the world's problems, followed by running her problems out of her, and sitting in the stillness that dissolved all problems, she had some time left over to find something else to do for herself.

That's when she decided it was time to create something that came from inside of her. She took a class that took her back to the time when she had called herself a creative, and she learned how to use pieces of the world around her to create a beautiful piece of her own. Time was spent picking up what the trees had dropped and looking up at one of the buildings that had always stood tall in front of her. She made those pieces white before turning them into her vision of the other. Creating one piece that connected the two lives she had in her one city.

With all the time in the world to create a new life, the girl took some time out to make a new friend. She was a girl who kept herself as pure as the color white. This was the one who had knocked on the floor of their work for her luck. They hadn't been friends when they'd sat at opposite ends of the same work, but they could be friends now that they didn't have that work between them. The girl would have gotten close to her back then, but this one wouldn't let her back when she was working herself to death. They could now be close friends outside of the place that hadn't worked out for the girl.

She told her new friend who kept herself pure about her life. The girl told this friend that she was spending some of her time, while sitting still, thinking about the parts of her life that were always breaking. She listened when the girl told her about a song that spoke to her. The one with the line that sang out how sadness could find you when you were young, then wait, only to come back so it could say that it had won. Beyond that, the girl wasn't thinking about what had been broken way back when. She only wanted to think through her breaks at work. Knowing it broke her because she worked too hard, she was starting to see how she was the one to blame for that. Without looking at why, she thought she finally knew what to do. She had to stop herself. This friend heard everything she said to her. She understood the girl wasn't working because she had to spend this time working on herself, so she could stop letting work break her.

Around now is when the girl met the good-looking man who sat down on a bench next to hers. She had seen him once before, sitting a few benches over, and had noticed how good he looked while he sat there. They hadn't talked then, but they talked now. They talked for a good hour and it felt like they'd talked for hours before that. He left, leaving the girl with the hope that they would get to talk again. She didn't have to wait long. They found each other, sitting on their benches, a few days later. They talked a lot that day, and then he asked her to talk some more, one night.

They met for a drink early the week after, and the girl let herself look at this man, who looked so good, without looking too deep. They talked about her life spent running from dream to dream. He liked the sound of her, and she liked the sounds he made. The man, who had been settled there for years, had left behind the work that he didn't love any longer, to follow his dream. He was spending his time creating beauty, singing and playing the sounds he wrote. The girl, who was searching for her new dream, liked the hope she felt when she looked at him.

After that first night, they spent some time together across a few weeks. They would meet in the middle of their days, spent dreaming up new lives, to talk while sitting on the stoops of other people's lives. They spent a few of their nights talking, before he would circle all of her in his arms. It felt good to be wrapped up this tight and get swept up again. The girl, who needed to believe in dreams again, didn't let herself look deep enough to see that this wasn't a good one. It was only a quick glimmer of light, just like the fly he cupped in his hands to show her its fire that first night they spent talking. She should have seen that they wouldn't be lit up for long when he couldn't catch the next one, the next night they went out together.

WHO BROKE THE GIRL?

☆
## WHEN THE LIGHT WENT OUT

By the time she saw the truth in him, it was almost too late for her. She had started to hope for more, and he could feel that, so he told her how he felt. That's when she heard – "I'm sad all of the time." The words that would have stopped someone else didn't stop the girl who knew what sadness felt like. The girl, who wanted to work at helping people, wanted to help him feel happy. She should have wanted to make herself happy. Instead of looking at that and seeing everything she would have to work through to get there, it was easier for her to keep seeing him, and try to help him.

She had gone down this road before without stopping, and she didn't stop now, but she did throw up enough blocks to stop them. The girl still wanted to see him, but they started to see each other less. She was around less on the weekends, now that she was going all the way back out to the end to find her balance by the water with her two friends. She was around less during the week now that she had decided to let other people pay her to stay in her home, while she lived with her friends.

He was asking to see her less even when she was around. The girl, who had been happy sitting on a bench and giving herself over to her dreams, was turning off what was inside of her that had led to their connection. Worry over the life she would lose if she didn't start working was taking her over, and she had stopped looking up a new dream. The work she had done for too long was pulling her back. She was afraid to be new again, so she gave up on changing. The man, who couldn't give up on his one dream, didn't want her worries in his life. She didn't share much of them with him, but the energy of them was coming off of her. So she got lucky, again, and he made the choice to stop seeing her. This man, who had said he was sad, said he wanted to be on his own. She still hadn't found enough of her own power to be the one who made the choice to leave him, but she had found enough to let him go when he made his choice.

They said goodbye after he used cold words to tell her what he wanted. He didn't want to date one girl when there was always another one around the next corner and could meet one anywhere in this city that was full of them. This man, who looked good on the surface, said there wasn't anything in her to hold his interest any longer. He wanted to turn the next corner to see the next girl. She knew he couldn't see who she was, so the girl walked away with her luck. Turning the corner, with his sadness behind her, made her feel good. She was starting to win out over sadness when losing a man who was sad didn't make her sad.

The girl didn't crumble over him, but by now the balance she'd found in her stillness was crumbling. She hadn't thought she could fall this low again and be filled with so much worry over finding a work that would pay for her life. After she stopped looking up at the light shining down on her, she started looking backwards, thinking she was moving herself forward. All of her time over the next few months was spent working hard to find places to talk to about how hard she could work for them. She found them and they talked for hours.

Giving up on the hope of a new dream, she thought she was making her life easier by going back to the work she'd been doing, where she'd already earned her spot. She couldn't give up what she had to to make something new happen. The girl hadn't forgotten while she sat still that her old work had never let her sit still, but she thought she was different enough now to make it different. Only, it was taking so long to find it that the wait, just like before, was pounding all hope out of her.

She talked to one person after the next, at one place after the next; looking for the work she knew she was good at. They all liked her and wanted her to come back to talk to the next person. She got higher and higher, until she had talked to all the people who needed to hear from her for them to hire her. She talked to a lot of people at a lot of places, but there was one place she talked to that she'd always dreamed of working at back when this had been her only dream.

She wanted to work at that place now, hoping it would help her find her way back to believing in this dream again. The girl got close, but she didn't get it; not remembering that a decision had to be made before everything would fall into place. She could pretend, even to herself, but she couldn't make herself want this type of work again. Her voice spoke the words she knew they all wanted to hear, about how much she loved this work, but there wasn't any truth for her words to stand on. Inside, she had already given up on this dream that had dropped her.

During this time that she felt like a failure, her friendship with the friend who hadn't let her go turned on her. The friend had left her work and her city behind, for a time, to be with the father she was losing. Once she returned, it took her less time to find work than it was taking the girl, since she was fine taking work that didn't matter to her. They had stood by each other when neither was working, but now that the girl was giving off worry they couldn't be good friends to each other. Their friendship wasn't as close now, even though they were living close. They each had too many worries to help the other out.

## WHO BROKE THE GIRL?

When they spoke, they could never connect with what the other was saying, so they spoke less.

Before they stopped speaking altogether, the friend told the girl she could come stay while she let other people live in her place. The girl came, but their bad energy drove her out quickly. She didn't feel good there, feeling how her friend didn't like having her there. She couldn't handle having her so close. The girl, who was feeling the weight of her worries, couldn't handle feeling like she was weighing someone down. Then her pride kicked in when her friend told her she couldn't stay. She felt like she was being kicked while down, which made her too hurt to stay friends with this one any longer. So the two friends let go of each other now that they couldn't handle being close to one another.

The only thing the girl could understand anymore was that she needed to work. Not so that her life would matter, but so that she could pay for the life she thought she wanted. After she got kicked, she went to live in the second room of her sister-friend's home. They liked living together, and the money the girl paid helped her friend keep her life going. She was there for two months longer than she wanted to be while strangers lived where she wanted to get back to. This friend was becoming an even closer sister, but the girl wanted her life back. She'd spoken to so many places, over so many months, that had made her think she was closing in on it, but each opportunity had disappeared on her. Finding work was taking too long. She had enjoyed sitting by herself, but she wanted to sit in one place with other workers again. She had enjoyed creating her own beautiful piece, but she wanted to help make beautiful pieces of work that the world would see again. She still needed to work on something that would be good, she hadn't given up on that, but she was losing hope that she would ever find it.

The family that had been supportive her last time out of work tried to reassure her. They told her she would find something soon enough. She couldn't hear them, but by then she couldn't hear much of what they said to her. She tried to stop feeling this way, but her feelings for them had turned. She still spoke to her mother, but she could barely speak to the father who had been the first man to bring fear into her life. He could feel her anger towards him, and he became even gentler back. He kept trying, too hard for her, to get the love he couldn't feel coming off her any longer. Every silent plea he sent out brought down more weight on her, and it pushed her away from him even further. Every time she went home she hoped she would feel different, but every time she felt herself grow colder. Her life that was breaking apart was breaking them.

It had started to go bad between them when her work had started to scare her. She hadn't seen the connection; she had just seen that she couldn't connect to him any longer. It came on slowly, and then slowly got worse. Now that she was out of work the pain inside of her that work had brought up to the surface was freezing any words she had for him. She wanted to stop the cold space growing between them, but she couldn't handle what she was feeling. Blaming him for everything she was starting to remember was coming between them, and she couldn't stop that blame now that it had started. Things were bad, and it would only get worse between them.

Before it got to that she kept her mind focused on working hard to find good work. Her fear of not working at all had taken over, and that's when she went to talk to the people at the next place she would work. She met one over coffee first thing one morning. He reminded her of the mad man that she had liked before, and she liked this one now. He had the same kind of stomping energy. They liked each other right away, and he told her to come in right away to meet with the creative leader of the place he managed. One known by everyone in the industry they worked in as someone who led good creative.

She went in the next day to meet for a few minutes. She voiced what she was thinking; she liked his work and that was all that mattered to her. That's all she had to say to him. He didn't ask her if she had any questions, but even if he had she wouldn't have asked any. The girl had too much fear of not working to ask the questions she didn't want answered. The answers that she knew would keep her from taking this work. She could see just by looking around that this place had little hope of surviving. If she had heard the truth then she would have been forced to make the right choice and decline to work there. Her hopelessness had brought a hopeless work into her life, and her fear made her forget to walk away from something that wasn't any good for her.

So she kept her worries to herself and started to work there a few days later. She had walked right in to the end of this work. She could see the first week there that this wasn't going to last for long. What she had been hired to do was already on its way out the first day she walked in. Everyone had been working hard, just like everyone does in this line of work, and what they had made before she got there was good. The people who paid them had liked what they created, but then people higher than them decided it wasn't right for them. So by the time she got there they had already started pushing them to create the work the way they told them. A way that everyone there knew wouldn't turn out any good. So the girl was back, on day one, doing work she didn't believe in.

Even though the work wasn't good any longer she could see the people around her were good at creating. They all worked hard and made it as good as they could. She started to like working there, even though she had already seen the end that was coming. The man who had led a lot of good work stood up to the people hurting their work. She had never seen that done before and she liked him for it. He drove his workers hard, but he made them laugh while he did it, so they still loved him. She laughed right along with everyone. He always told them about his life that had just broken apart while they worked hard on the

## WHO BROKE THE GIRL?

work that was getting broken. The girl felt for him, and she started to feel like he was her friend that she worked for.

Everything about this work was different from what she had done before. The girl was different. She didn't work herself too hard, and she let the young girl she led do what she was supposed to without her. She used her head to think through how to make the work smarter and the ones who paid them happier. Even though both were impossible. She worked closely with the two men who had hired her and the one man there paid to be a thinker. They all liked how she thought. There were times when they pushed her to work harder, but now she pushed back. She wasn't going to give her life over to work, not like she had before.

Then the end she had seen coming started. The work they were being forced to make got worse. They talked about what to do, and they all agreed that they would rather give up this work than do something that wasn't any good. This dream had started to flicker back on for her, and she didn't want to lose it over bad work, not again. The girl, who had just been out of work, told them – "I'd rather not work at all than do work I don't believe in."

Everyone agreed, but they didn't back away. They all still needed the money this work was paying them. The only thing that changed was that the best creatives were taken off her work. After a few months of making what no one liked, the decision to end it was made for them. The people who paid them decided to take away the work. They didn't know how bad their directions had been, but they decided they could go in this direction on their own. The girl knew this meant she might be out, but she was glad to see the last of them and that work.

WHO BROKE THE GIRL?

☆
## WHAT THEY WANTED FROM HER

By now the leader who made her laugh liked her because she made him laugh. So even though there wasn't any work for her to do, they kept her. They would have let go of the one she managed, who had no work to do now either, but that one went away on her own. The girl stayed and tried to help them win new work that she could then work on. It's not what she liked to do, but she knew she had to stay there and do that while she looked for work somewhere else. She wasn't sure she should leave, but she was sure she didn't want to end up with no work, and no way to pay for the life she had gone back to living on her own. Then, the two leaders brought in a third, one who was supposed to help them win more work. Right when he started they all started working together to try to win something they all wanted to work on. It was for good people who wanted to do a good thing for the world, and it would be good creative work.

While they were doing that, everything good at this work came to an end. With this third leader there now, there was no room for the girl's thoughts. The creative leader that had liked what she had to say before couldn't hear her now. While they worked at winning this new work, he would only listen when this other man spoke. The girl sat in meetings with his back turned to her, and she looked at these two men that would only look at each other the whole time. She went from being treated like a leader to being treated like she was someone brand new to this work.

She spoke up but it didn't help her. The leader who she thought of as a friend said he heard her, but she could see he didn't understand her. He thought she was questioning herself. She wasn't doing that, but she was questioning him. In the next meeting she still couldn't get anyone to look over at her. The only difference was, on his way out the leader turned and told everyone – "That girl is one smart cookie." She flinched, embarrassed by what everyone must have thought. She didn't stop speaking up, and he didn't start looking over, but he kept calling her a smart cookie. This was the type of work where everyone spoke freely, and she could handle any words he spoke to her, but she couldn't handle not being allowed to speak. She kept pushing to be heard and kept getting pushed over.

## WHO BROKE THE GIRL?

While she wasn't being heard, she was being pushed to work harder. The girl did what they needed her to, even though it was work she wasn't supposed to be doing any longer. She did it because there was no one else to. If she'd known she would have to go back to doing this work, like she'd done years earlier, then she would have chosen to start her life over with that new dream of helping others. Instead, she was stuck doing this, working hard for men that treated her like she shouldn't speak and should jump to do whatever they told her. It wasn't any harder than she'd worked before, but she started to break, like before. Not from the work, but from the way she was being treated.

She tried to hide it, but she knew she wasn't doing a good job at that. The leader still wanted to treat her like a friend and would turn to talk to her like one outside of those meetings. She kept trying to speak up in them, but in there he kept stopping her. So the girl who had never been good at faking her feelings stopped laughing, which made him stop liking her. Knowing she would be out soon if she didn't start up again, she worked to push down the pain she was feeling, and she knew how weak she looked to them. They couldn't see how much strength it took to keep everything going.

She worked straight through the days and late into the nights. Running to keep the work going, right alongside the young ones who were working the same long hours. Working the way young ones work, the way she had always worked since she was young. Then it came time for the last day before they showed their work to the people they wanted to hire them. The day that started early, that she didn't stop moving through. The day he drove her to move faster so the creatives that would be speaking in the meeting could go home and rest. It didn't matter that she was also speaking in that meeting and wouldn't be able to go home until late, before coming back in too early the next morning. The girl had made her choice, back when she'd made the choice to work hard at this role that no one thought mattered. He was just confirming the choice she'd made to move herself back to second.

They won the work and everyone smiled, but the girl still couldn't force one. She knew it didn't mean she was staying since it wasn't paying them enough to pay her, and she still wasn't laughing, so she asked the leader what his plans were for her. While getting up to walk away, he said – "I don't know, but it's not looking good." Then he came back over a few minutes later to tell her he liked her, so he would keep her. Then a few days later he looked over to tell her – "I'm trying so hard not to fire you." The girl, who had lived her life swinging between extremes, was trying hard to keep her balance. She told him – "Do what you have to do." She needed to get paid, but she couldn't live like this, and she wanted to go.

She was too scared of not having money, to keep her life going, to leave without another work to go to. So the girl forced herself to start laughing again, even though she didn't find anything funny. She forced out a smile at all the words that weren't supposed to be said at work. Words that hadn't bothered her when she could choose to laugh, but now that she had no choice they became words she couldn't stand. She let the leader, who hugged and touched everyone, hug and touch her every day. Along with the touching came any words he chose to say. He did the same to everyone, but she didn't like it and would softly voice it, making sure to keep herself laughing.

At all the places she'd worked before, she'd never felt like this. She'd always been taken seriously for her work, without being touched, and with only a few words thrown around that made her feel any discomfort. This way of working pained her. She tried to act like she wasn't bothered, but it was killing her. Not because she was worried that the touching, done out in the open, was done to bring on any more. He did it because he knew he could, and he liked seeing how long it would take her to say – "Stop touching me." The power he yielded over her was crushing.

While she forced herself to live with that, the power that had connected her to her father went out. All the gentle words between them were disappearing. She still couldn't see the controlling connection between her past and this time she was now living. She could only feel how she had no control over her life, and that led her to break off the last of the connection she had to him. She'd stopped speaking to him whenever she went to see them and soon they stopped seeing each other when she went there. It hurt her to do this, but she was hurting too much, and it hurt her even more to be around him. She wouldn't be able to bring herself close to him again until much later, after all her pain hit her at once, and she could see what needed to be cleared out.

Before she did that, and while she did this, everything she was forcing herself to do to keep this work going was working. She knew she could stay as long as she kept doing it, but she couldn't stand it for much long. She couldn't stay somewhere she couldn't speak and had to be touched. While she stayed quiet over the next few months, her heart screamed. All she wanted was to do good work, so she looked for a place where she could do that. This place that had made her feel the flicker of her dream again had turned into a nightmare.

While she was looking to leave, a new boy started. He'd just arrived from the other side of the country. A little older than her, he didn't seem too old since he was another one who never wanted to grow old. She didn't think twice about this boy and didn't think he thought twice about her. They hit it off right away though, and she felt sure they would be friends, but she never thought they would be anything more than friendly. They stayed friendly as they worked closely on the new work that had been won.

Then one night, after a late night of working, they decided to have a drink and talk about work. They drank while they talked, and then without her ever deciding to they started kissing. The girl was doing something she didn't understand with this boy she had never thought of before that night. She would never know what it was that they shared since they never discussed it, and neither told anyone that there was now something more than work between them.

While they shared whatever that was they kept sharing their work. He was good at his, and she was good at hers, so they worked well together. In their meetings with the men that were paying them they spoke off of one another. Before and after these meetings this boy would always ask her opinion on the work he was creating. She could speak her mind with him and could hear how he liked to listen to what she had to say. She liked working with him and whatever it was they were doing outside of work. Only, she didn't like hiding. She told herself it would only be while they worked in this one place together, which she hoped wouldn't be for much longer.

When they met outside of work there wasn't any hiding. They liked kissing each other, and they would stop to kiss on the streets while they were walking, for anyone to see. Neither their kissing nor their work together lasted for long. By now, she'd found what was going to let her leave this one behind. She had asked all the hard questions this time, and even though this new place didn't have a lot of work, she believed in the people there and in what they were telling her. They all had a strong hope that they could grow this place into the dream they all shared. She was going to be a real leader now. With people she could do good work with, while laughing without being force. Her hope for this dream lit up bright again.

The boy she was seeing was sad she was leaving him to do this work without her, but he told her he was happy for her. He also told her he still couldn't tell anyone about them. He had a fear that the man, who was still his leader, wouldn't like him because of what he was doing with her. The girl didn't like what she was hearing, but she thought she could keep seeing him, and he would stop seeing it that way after she left. Then she found out she wouldn't see him for a little while, since he was taking himself back to where he'd come from.

The boy, who had just moved there, wasn't saying so, but he hadn't really decided if he was staying. He said he was going back to pack up his stuff from his last life, but she could hear the truth he wasn't saying. He was going back to decide if he should stay there. At first they stayed in touch. Then the boy, who couldn't make a decision, lost touch. The day he was supposed to come back came and went with no word from him. He didn't say anything, so she didn't either. The girl, who had gotten used to speaking her mind to this boy every day, was hurt. She wasn't crushed, but the loss was enough to make her feel some pain. He had dropped her out of nowhere. She knew he would come back at some point, but she made the choice right then to stop what they were doing.

She wasn't going to live her life pushed over to second or hidden away any longer. She had done that enough for a lifetime. When he finally decided to get in touch she stood by her decision. She told him that whatever it was they had shared had been nice, but it wasn't enough for her at this point in her life. The girl felt her power in making that choice and not waiting for him to tell her what it was that he had decided. She was done with him, and she'd already decided to go out with someone new to help her move away from this small pain. She'd met a new guy even before the boy who couldn't make a decision had tried to come back. She had no idea that this decision to move on to this guy, who she called kid, would change her entire life.

WHO BROKE THE GIRL?

☆
## CONCLUSION: AN END TO HER START

She liked what she saw as soon as she first saw him, but she couldn't think about him too much at first. She needed to close the last door before she could see through the next. Even though she wasn't thinking about him that much, she couldn't help but start to feel how much more she wanted to see him than she wanted to see the other boy come back. He wanted to see her even more than that, and he told her how he'd never met anyone like her. She couldn't help but let all of his goodness into her life. The kid, who had started off as a distraction, quickly lit her best dream up with the brightest shine she'd ever seen.

He made her shake with laughter whenever he spoke, and he would break out into his own laughter with whatever she came back with. He had more good in him than there was in anyone she'd ever known, and he could see straight through to every side of her. He saw the best in her; the parts she'd always known were there but couldn't hold on to, the ones he was now bringing out in her. They liked everything they saw in each other, and they gave everything they had without asking for anything back. She felt weightless when she was with him, and he didn't have to do anything for her to have the happiest time of her life. He brought her more safety and comfort than she'd ever known. He was pure good, and the two felt pure happiness together.

This time, that was the happiest time of her life, wouldn't last long enough. He never wanted to hurt her, even though what he would have to do to save his own life would bring all the pain she'd ever felt across her entire life up to crash down on her, all at once. He had to leave her alone with that pain because he had his own to manage, and he had to learn how to stand on his own for himself and for the one that he called kid. When he left her it would feel like the worst thing ever to her, but it was the only right thing he could have done for either of them. He had come to realize he couldn't give her what she deserved, not at that point in his life, and he wouldn't take from her without giving. The girl came into this man's fractured life too early for them to build the life they wanted together. This would turn into her hardest lesson yet, pulling all the hard lessons of her life together to be dealt with, once and for all.

At first she crumbled, curling up tight around her pain, stumbling through the clouds of grief that surrounded her. She found anything she could to distract her. She saw other boys, but she couldn't see anyone clearly while looking at them and couldn't make a connection. She turned to all her friends, and they all turned up for her, but she couldn't talk the pain out of her. She pushed herself to work, and she leaned on the people there that she'd come to depend on. She couldn't stop leaning. Nothing shined as bright as before, and she started to wonder if it was better that way, to live a life that couldn't hurt one with its dullness.

Just when she started to accept that she had lost the best, and to believe she would never see the best in herself again, things turned worse on her. She lost the work that she'd thought was going to be her best one yet. They hadn't known the truth in their words back when they told her it was safe to work there, and they now had to let go of all of them. The work that was distracting her from her pain was being forced out of her life. The girl would be left alone to suffer all day, every day, and that scared her enough to finally wake up.

This loss was a loud call for her to put a stop to her long run and teach herself the right way to live. There wasn't a lower bottom for her to drop to, and she knew she had to stop herself from ever dropping again. It was time to learn how to be happy despite anything, not because of something. She was being forced to look deeply at her entire life and see the lessons that had been driving her from one break to the next.

The next year of her life would be spent clear of all distractions, so she could face what was inside of her. Seeing herself clearer than ever, she would come to understand how her breaks, those that had happened so early, had driven her to keep breaking herself on all the broken things she kept bringing into her life. All the people she could have turned away from but instead kept trying to help, until their breaks drove them to leave her life. All the places she had chosen to work too hard for, breaking herself against them until she could do nothing more than break off from them. The girl finally helped herself and started to work on clearing out everything broken, so she could keep her balance and see her own beauty. She began to believe in how much she mattered for who she was, and to feel the power that was deep inside of her. Finding the happiness that was there for her life, the one that she deserved to put first.

After their happiness was taken away, the one that was better than any she'd known before him, the girl woke up and learned – "I was the one breaking myself all along." From breaking to healing she made herself whole, so her happiness could now come from the inside out, and stay with her no matter what came along to hit her life. She had faith that the kid, who was the best, was turning himself into the strong man that he deserved to become, and she knew

## WHO BROKE THE GIRL?

she was becoming the strong woman that she had always wanted to be. She would keep her hope alive that when it was right for both of them then they would meet again. Shining in her strength, she knew it was her time to make the right dreams real, the ones her soul had always wanted, and that she hadn't known she deserved before.

CRISTINA COSTANTINO

☆
## ABOUT THE AUTHOR

Raised by working class parents in an Italian immigrant enclave of Syracuse NY, Cristina Costantino attended Syracuse University with a dual major in Communications and International Relations. Starting off as a graphic designer in NYC, she then moved on to a 12-year advertising career in client management; while moving herself down to Charlotte, over to Milan, back to NYC and across to London. After leaving London she took a 4-month break to backpack across SE Asia. Then settled down roots in the one city she always called home – NYC.